Date Due

MAY 31			

BRODART   Cat. No. 23 233   Printed in U.S.A.

Str
Ab

Kay M

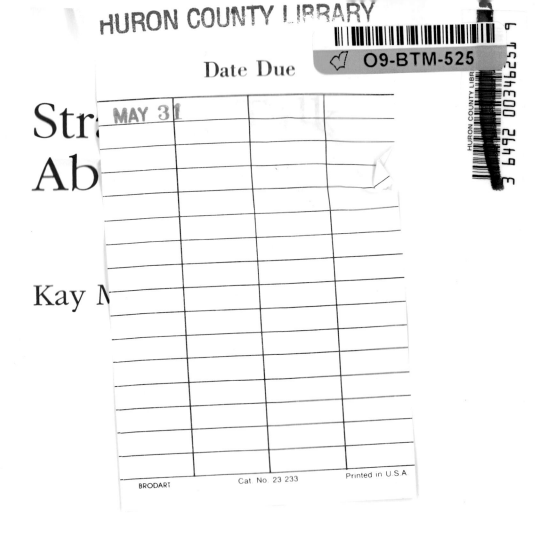

☑® Facts On File, Inc.

Straight Talk About Cults

Kay Marie Porterfield

☑® Facts On File, Inc.

Straight Talk About Cults

Facts On File, Inc.
11 Penn Plaza
New York NY 10001

Library of Congress Cataloging-in-Publication Data

Porterfield, Kay Marie.
Straight talk about cults / Kay Marie Porterfield.
    p.   cm.
  Includes bibliographical references and index.
  ISBN 0-8160-3750-7 (pbk) (alk. paper)
    1. Cults—United States—Controversial literature. 2. Cults—
United States—Juvenile literature. 3. Teenagers—United States—
Religious life. [1. Cults.] I. Title.
  BL2525.P67   1995
  291.9—dc20   94-37296

Facts On File books are available at special discounts when purchased in bulk quantities for businesses, associations, institutions or sales promotions. Please contact our Special Sales Department in New York at 212/967-8800 or 800/322-8755.

You can find Facts On File on the World Wide Web at
http://www.factsonfile.com

Cover design by Smart Graphics

Printed in the United States of America

MP FOF 10 9 8 7 6 5 4 3 2 1

This book is printed on acid-free paper.

About the Straight Talk About . . . series:

The Straight Talk About . . . books provide young adult readers with the most factual, up-to-date information available. Recognizing that the teen years are a time of growth and transition, the authors aim not to dispense any easy answers or moral judgments but to help young people clarify a number of issues and difficult choices and to consider the consequences of their decisions. Each book is throughly indexed and contains a directory of resources.

Contents

Other Books by the Author:

Coping with an Alcoholic Parent

Coping with Codependency

Teenage Perspectives: Focus on Addictions

*Blind Faith: Recognizing and Healing from
Dysfunctional Religious Groups*

1

Cults—No Simple Truth

On a quiet Sunday in early March of 1993, federal agents surrounded the group of buildings where David Koresh and his followers lived in Waco, Texas. The agents from the Bureau of Alcohol, Tobacco and Firearms believed that members of Koresh's church, the Branch Davidians, had stockpiled 8,000 pounds of ammunition and enough parts to build hundreds of automatic weapons and that they planned to use these guns against innocent people.

Almost as soon as the agents were in position, shots rang from the walls of the compound. By the time this gunfire ended in a standoff three-quarters of an hour later, four government agents lay dead and fifteen were wounded. Koresh claimed that ten of his flock had died, including his two-year-old daughter. He also claimed that the bloodbath proved that the prophesies he had been making for years had come true.

Koresh, who called himself Christ, had preached that his followers needed to get ready for a battle with unbelievers that would signal the end of the world. He made them watch war movies and put them through his own version of basic training. Members were deprived of food in order to prepare for a possible famine. They couldn't buy their own food because they had given all their money to their leader in order to join the group. They spent their days working hard in isolation. When they were finished, they studied the Bible until late into the night. Even watching television to learn what was going on beyond the walls of the compound was forbidden.

When Koresh's Branch Davidians declared they were fighting a holy war and refused to surrender, the U.S. government sent more than 400 federal agents to Waco. They were helped by SWAT teams, local police, and National Guard tanks. For two months they pleaded and bargained with David Koresh. They also broadcast loud music and shone bright lights into the group's compound to force the ninety-some members who remained to give up from sheer exhaustion. Instead of causing Koresh's followers to give up, these tactics made them resist surrender even harder. Because they believed that the government forces were evil and that the world soon would end anyway, they felt they had nothing to gain by giving up.

In May 1993, after hearing reports that children in the Waco compound had been beaten and sexually abused, the U.S. attorney general Janet Reno ordered a full-scale assault on the buildings that had housed Koresh's flock. Shortly after the attack was launched, the buildings burst into flames. Some witnesses described the scene as a hellish inferno; it completely destroyed the buildings that had housed the Branch Davidians. Government agents were convinced that David Koresh had set the fire in order to prove his forecasts about doomsday. When the ashes finally cooled, investigators found the remains of eighty-six bodies. Many of the victims were women and children. For Koresh's followers, at least, this holy war with unbelievers *had* truly signaled the end of the world.

Cults: No Simple Truth

Most of the time we take little notice of small groups of people who play follow-the-leader and behave in ways that appear strange to us. When we see Hare Krishnas dancing in the streets or are asked for money by a Unification Church member, or Moonie, we may react with bemusement or mild irritation. These people act differently, but they seem harmless enough. Of course, we tell ourselves, *we'd* never believe what they do or make spectacles of ourselves, but the Constitution guarantees religious freedom. Citizens of this country are free to believe what they want.

When a David Koresh sets fire to his followers or a Jim Jones convinces more than 900 of his flock to commit mass suicide in Jonestown, however, the dangers of cults are magnified.

That is certainly what happened when in the early morning of October 5, 1994, forty-eight members of a group called the Order of the Solar Temple were found dead in a farmhouse and three chalets in the Swiss countryside. Five more bodies of group members were discovered in a small town near Montreal, Canada. Although many of the victims in Switzerland had been badly burned in a fire that appeared to have been started deliberately, others were unscathed because of a malfunction in the mechanism thought to have been used to start the blaze. Those people were dressed in red, black, and golden ceremonial robes and had met their deaths lying in a circle near an altar containing a cross and a rose. Twenty of the bodies had bullet wounds, most often to the head; many others had plastic bags over their heads. A local judge ruled that the deaths were mass suicide. Many people believe that the victims were inspired to take their own lives by Luc Jouret, the group's charismatic leader.

When cults make the headlines, many people question the right of religious freedom. Some people, however, tend to label *any* group that believes differently than they do a cult. They feel threatened by others who don't fit into their view of society. The truth about cults is not a simple, black/white matter.

Appearances Can Be Deceiving

Audrey's* mom began paying for sessions with a psychic counselor soon after her husband's death. The man called himself Master X, wore expensive, designer business suits and claimed to work with spirit guides who passed messages to and from Audrey's father. Audrey's mom said that seeing the psychic made her feel better. She seemed happier now that she had an interest in life, but soon the monthly counseling sessions became twice-weekly in addition to a Sunday morning "spirit service." When the psychic raised his fee, he put a real strain on the family budget. To make matters worse, Audrey's mother began consulting the man about every decision that faced her. When he asked her to donate a large portion of her husband's insurance settlement to the church he was starting, she didn't hesitate. When she found a lump in her breast, she refused to get a mammogram, insisting the psychic could heal her if she had cancer.

Audrey, fearful of the psychic's control over their lives, voiced her concerns that he might be heading a cult, but her mother became defensive. "Don't be silly," she replied. "I have a college degree, and I know exactly what I'm doing. I know I couldn't possibly be part of a cult. My spiritual teacher is helping, not hurting me. Respect my right to do what's right for myself."

---

*Unless both a first and last name are given, all of the stories of teenagers in this book are *composites*—fictional portraits of teenagers that make use of real elements of teenagers' lives.

Is Audrey's concern over her mother misplaced? Even if Master X doesn't have special powers, he's making Audrey's mother happy. He dresses and acts like a successful businessman. He holds church services, and his clients include wealthy professionals in the community. The only thing that seems strange about him is his name. Audrey's mom could be involved in a damaging cult, or she might be simply the victim of a crafty con-artist preying on her grief.

From the time he was a baby, William was raised in the traditional Indian ways of his father and grandfather. Once a week friends and relatives gather in their backyard to hold a purification ceremony in a small sweatlodge his dad and uncles built. After they finish praying in the lodge, they form a circle and smoke a pipe similar to the sacred pipe that was given 'to their people thousands of years ago. Burning sage, singing spiritual songs, and preparing to participate in the annual Sundance back in South Dakota are a normal part of William's daily life.

The next door neighbors, however, are convinced the family's spiritual beliefs are anything *but* normal. In fact, one woman has called the police several times to complain that a cult of satanists has been using drugs and participating in demonic rituals across her back fence. She says she fears for her safety and has convinced the minister of her church to preach sermons aimed at driving William's family out of the neighborhood.

Are William's neighbor and his classmates justified in their fears that a sinister cult is taking over the neighborhood? William's family does do many things that set them apart from their neighbors. They sing in a language their neighbors can't understand to music made with drums. They don't attend church on Sunday. Or maybe the neighbors are being closed-minded about a tradition that has been practiced for centuries and are persecuting William and his family.

Defining exactly what a cult is and what it isn't can be tricky. Even though the term *cult* is often used as a put-down, it wasn't meant to be originally. The Latin word *cultus,* from which the word *cult* comes, simply means a group of people who share intense devotion to a person, place, thing, or idea. Sometimes *cult* is still used that way in our language. When fans focus their lives around a rock star or a popular sports figure, these fans are often termed a *cult following.* Frenzied fanatics of baseball are sometimes jokingly called the *baseball cult.* If you spend hours listening to recordings of the 1960s rock group The Doors some people might say you belong to a cult, too—the Jim Morrison cult. Most of the time, though, when people talk about a cult, they are speaking of an organized group of people who are devoted to a leader, more often than not a *religious* leader.

For years psychologists, sociologists, and cult researchers have struggled to come up with a precise definition for the term *cult.* Not all of these people are in agreement. The best they have been able to do is to come up with lists of characteristics that cults share. Three of these characteristics are common to the checklists of most cult researchers.

Cult Characteristics

Cults, whether they help or harm their members, possess three distinct characteristics:

1. a living, charismatic leader who claims to have ultimate wisdom,
2. an authoritarian power structure, and
3. rigid boundaries.

If a group has only one or even two of these characteristics, it might not be a cult. When a group possesses all three, it most certainly is a cult. Even though the group might not be a danger to its members or those who surround them, it has the *potential* to damage people.

Charismatic Leaders

According to John Hochman, M.D., assistant clinical professor of psychiatry at the U.C.L.A. School of Medicine in Los Angeles, to qualify as a cult, a group must have a living, charismatic leader, an especially charming person who speaks in a convincing manner and draws people to him- or herself. Leaders of religious cults usually claim to be gods or to be God's exclusive messengers on earth. They teach that they are infallible, or make no mistakes, and that they possess special talents or gifts that ordinary human beings don't have. Like Master X, they may claim to communicate with the spirits of the deceased or to have special healing powers. Some tell followers that they can read minds or send their spirits outside of their bodies to keep tabs on others.

Believing these things about themselves and convincing other people of them doesn't necessarily make cult leaders dangerous. Leaders become holy terrorists when they are power-hungry, greedy, or violent in addition to believing that they are God's exclusive messenger on earth. Like David Koresh, such leaders may even decide to arm cult members and fight a holy war. Given a charismatic leader's powers of persuasion and followers' belief that the leader can do no wrong, the leader can often convince or manipulate followers to go against their previous values about what is right and wrong. People who would otherwise never think of hurting another person may become willing to torture or even kill when they are under the sway of a charismatic leader.

In Park County, Montana, Elizabeth Clare Prophet currently teaches that the world will end any day. Like Koresh, she manipulates her membership through fear. She has gathered at least 2,000 followers around her in this rural Montana county and has sold them space in bomb shelters so they can survive the end of the world. She has also ordered her group, the Church Universal and Triumphant (sometimes called the Summit Lighthouse), to stockpile semiautomatic rifles and assault rifles. Her church has so many guns and so much ammunition and explosives that a state representative has urged the governor of Montana to declare a state of emergency because of it.

Many charismatic cult leaders also believe that they have the right to use violence to keep followers obedient. Because they consider themselves and their actions to be holy and therefore above the law, these leaders will resort to force in order to get their way. In 1977, Paul Morantz, a Los Angeles lawyer, won a lawsuit brought by a husband and wife who claimed they had been brainwashed and imprisoned in Synanon, the drug treatment program founded by charismatic leader Chuck Dederich. Three weeks later when Morantz put his hand in his mailbox, a 4 ½-foot diamondback rattlesnake sunk its fangs into him. Police later discovered that Synanon members put the snake there to teach the lawyer a lesson. Although no direct orders for this action from Dederich were uncovered, the founder of Synanon had established the belief among members that they must protect him and his reputation at all costs.

Jeffrey Lundgren, the leader of The Family, a cult based on 19th-century Mormon (Latter Day Saints) teachings, was willing to resort to murder to convince followers of his divinity. He encouraged his small congregation, not only to obey him, but to help eliminate those who didn't believe in him, saying that "killing sinners is not murder, but an act of kindness aimed at earning a place in heaven." In 1991, cult members were accused of killing a family of five who did not believe that Lundgren was holy. The family was getting ready to leave the cult when Lundgren ordered them to be tied up, gagged, and shot to death. Police discovered their bodies buried under a barn on the farm in Ohio where the cult was based. They also found evidence that the group was prepared to kill hundreds of other people to ensure their own salvation. Lundgren was convicted of five counts of aggravated murder and kidnapping.

Authoritarian Power Structure

Once people join a cult, they are expected to obey its leader without question. Cult leaders establish rules and regulations governing everything from what members can and cannot eat to whom they can speak with or what they can read. Some cult leaders even tell followers whom they can marry and how many children they can have. Followers may be told how to spend every minute of the day. The strictest groups even try to control their members' thoughts and feelings. People who need a rigid schedule and who want to be told what to do may not be bothered by these conditions, but most of us would be emotionally harmed by living such a controlled life. When we give up our independence, we soon lose the ability to make decisions for ourselves. Once handing over our ability to control our lives becomes a habit, it is very difficult for us say to say no, especially to a charming and charismatic leader.

If a cult allows its members to disagree with its rules and to walk away from it when they feel they are being hurt or they disagree with cult teachings or practices, then members may resume their former lives without distress. The trouble is few cults allow members such freedom to think or to act. Dangerous cults insist that members remain unquestioning and obedient no matter what. If not, members are punished. Sometimes followers are even punished for showing their emotions, especially if those feelings include anger at the leader, confusion, or pain because of the harm being done to them.

Some cults, such as Jeffrey Lundgren's The Family, use harsh methods to enforce their strict regulations. Often it is not cult members themselves but their children who suffer the most. In 1991, federal officials arrested Eldridge Broussard, Jr., the charismatic leader of the Oregon- and

California-based Ecclesia Athletic Association along with seven of his followers and charged them with slavery and violating the rights of children. When Broussard's daughter stole food to eat, her father ordered members to beat her. They beat her to death. Federal investigators found that children aged three to eighteen had routinely been beaten and forced to be part of an "exhibition team" that ran long distances in order to raise money for the religious group. In the words of the federal indictment handed down against the association:

> The children who did not want to perform, who made mistakes and who did not fully comply with the defendants' [Broussard's followers'] orders were struck with long wooden paddles and whipped with razor straps, braided cords and rubber hoses. The children repeatedly were threatened with physical punishment and frequently were forced to watch other children being whipped and beaten.

Rigid Boundaries

Since the beliefs, practices, and values of cults are often very different from those that are considered usual in our society, cult members are often thought to be strange. Sometimes, especially if they dress in odd clothing or act in ways that readily mark them as being different, they are treated as outcasts by society and even by their own families. When these lines are drawn, people who belong to cults soon come to think that people who aren't a part of their group are enemies.

Cult leaders do everything they can to promote this extreme fear of outsiders as persecutors in order to get members to obey their rules. When the Church of Scientology came under investigation by the Internal Revenue Service, which doubted that the cult really qualified as a church, the organization declared war against the government agency. The group's illegal tactics in the past have included sending spies into the IRS and using bribery and blackmail so they could avoid paying taxes. Scientology leaders claim they have been unfairly persecuted and have hinted that they would stop at nothing to bring the agency to its knees. Because members of the group had been taught that the IRS is evil, there was no problem convincing them to break laws.

Many cult leaders teach their followers that they are superior to people who don't subscribe to the cult's teachings. Even though followers may be starved or beaten, they are told they are special people, a chosen few. This sense of being special further sets cult members apart from outsiders. That is one of the reasons why so many people chose to stay with David Koresh in the Branch Davidian compound despite the harsh conditions of their daily lives. The belief that they were saved and that all those outside the walls were sinners served as a reason to lay down their lives during the shootout. They felt that they were dying for a holy cause and that those they killed were inferior, unworthy of remaining alive.

Some leaders insist that members live in isolation, having nothing to do with others—even their own family members—because contact with the unconverted might corrupt them. Cult members go along with this demand because they feel superior to non-believers, and they also fear that leaving the group even for a day or two might spiritually doom them.

The isolation that comes from seeing the world outside as evil causes people in cults to become completely dependent on the group to meet their emotional needs for love, self-esteem, and belonging. The rigid boundaries of cults give members a closely shared identity and feelings of contentment and well-being as well as the illusion of safety and security. Because people who belong to cults are not exposed to outside people or ideas, their notion of reality changes to what cult leaders want them to believe and their minds are more easily controlled.

Cult or Religion?

One problem with finding an exact definition for the word *cult* is that many of today's dominant organized religious groups began as cults. Gathering around a charismatic leader, having an authoritarian power structure and possessing rigid boundaries are stages in the development of all religious movements. In fact, one cult researcher has defined cults as "first-generation religions." Some of these groups die out when their leader dies. Others, such as Scientology, retain their cult characteristics well after the death of their leader. Many times, though, a group outgrows cult practices when they are no longer needed for its survival. The cult then becomes accepted by society as a religion.

Judaism, Christianity, and Islam all grew out of tightly knit communities of believers with leaders who said their doctrines or teachings came directly from God. The Jewish people followed Moses who said he spoke to God in the form of a burning bush. Christians followed Jesus Christ who told them he was the Son of God. Islamic people were led by Mohammed who said the Koran, the Moslem holy book, was dictated by Allah. The disciples or followers of these religious leaders were extremely devoted, some so devoted, they were willing to lay down their lives for their faith.

Many of the practices of Judaism, Christianity, and Islam seemed shocking to those who didn't share them, and adherents of those religions were often persecuted. Because of persecution and isolation, bonds between members within each of these three religious groups became stronger. Many times believers were told to have nothing to do with outsiders. In order to survive as a group and spread their beliefs, followers often placed their lives under the complete control of their spiritual leaders.

According to the Committee on Psychiatry and Religion of the Group for the Advancement of Psychiatry, time and acceptance are necessary for a cult to be considered a religion. Today Judaism, Christianity, and Islam are viewed as established religions, not cults, because millions of people share the beliefs taught by these faiths. Although religious persecution for holding these beliefs has not ended in all parts of the world, in many places sheer numbers of followers guarantee freedom from persecution. The lives of most Jews, Christians, and Moslems are no longer totally controlled by their religious leaders because such control isn't necessary for the group's survival.

The process of groups changing from cults to established religions is still happening today. The Church of Christ, Scientist (Christian Science), Jehovah's Witnesses, and the Church of Jesus Christ of Latter Day Saints (Mormons) were all considered radical cults in the 1800s shortly after they were founded. Today conservative Christian groups still label these three groups as cults and call their members cult followers. Many people, however, would place Christian Scientists, Jehovah's Witnesses and Mormons in the same category as they do Catholics, Methodists, or Baptists. They consider these people to be members of established religions.

To make matters even more confusing, there are several types of religious cults. Some cults are also called *sects*. These are splinter groups that have broken away from an older, more established organization. For example, Koresh's Branch Davidians pulled away from the Seventh-Day Adventist Church. Many sects believe that the religions they have broken with have gone off-base. Their new religious practices and teachings are an attempt to return to what they believe to be a purer form of the organized group they have left. Not all sects are cults, because not all of them have the three cult characteristics discussed earlier.

Other cults are formed around a brand new belief, for example Scientology, which spreads the teachings of former science fiction writer L. Ron Hubbard. Sociologists who study cult movements call these organizations *new religious movements* or *NRMs*. A few of the new religious movements today include the Unification Church, or Moonies, The Church Universal and Triumphant, and groups that practice spiritualism or channeling.

Some groups that are said to be new religions are actually practicing old traditions that come from another culture or part of the world but are new to the dominant culture in North America today. The Hare Krishnas, Buddhists, and Wiccans (modern-day practitioners of pre-Christian European religions) fall into this category. Some of the "old" religions currently practiced by a relatively small number of people in this country are considered cults because they have a charismatic leader, an authoritarian power structure, and rigid boundaries, such as the Hare Krishnas and some Buddhist sects do.

Many of these old belief systems—be they Native American, Far Eastern, African, or European—have none of the cult characteristics mentioned earlier. They are mistakenly labeled as cults only because they are different from the religions most people in our culture currently practice. When people condemn spiritual beliefs and practices by calling them cults only because these forms of spirituality are unfamiliar, they run the risk of denying certain people their guaranteed right of religious freedom.

Some cults have religious practices similar to those of established religions and don't appear very different from what most people would consider normal. Leaders of these groups hold Sunday services and act like shrewd businessmen who could fit right into the corporate mainstream. Their followers are middle-class, well-educated people, but these leaders exercise almost total control over their daily lives. They even attempt to control members' thoughts. The followers, in turn, are fanatically devoted, giving large sums of money better spent on their families, obeying every order and narrowing their lives so that these leaders and their religious groups became their total focus.

Separating the Good Guys from the Bad Guys

Even if a religious organization can properly be called a cult, that doesn't mean it is a menace to its members or the world. Some cults are relatively harmless. They may even help the people who join them by giving them a sense of belonging and purpose in their lives. The cult group provides a feeling of family for members and helps them solve some of their problems.

Other cults, especially those centered around a greedy or power-hungry leader, hurt people who join them. The injury these organizations inflict ranges from emotional abuse to physical harm. Sometimes involvement with a cult can result in death as it did for so many of the Branch Davidians. Cults that emotionally, sexually or physically abuse their members are called *damaging, destructive, or dangerous cults* by the experts. The Cult Awareness Network, a national organization that monitors these groups, defines a destructive cult as "a group with a hidden agenda of power through deceptive recruitment and complete control of the minds and lives of its members."

Most of us would like to believe the myth that groups like the ones that spawned the tragedies in Switzerland, Canada, Waco, and Jonestown (where Jim Jones' followers committed mass suicide) are rare, but it is likely that right now a cult leader is quietly gathering followers and setting the stage for yet another tragedy that will unfold years from today. Because these leaders tend to be secretive about the inner workings of their groups and their membership, the number of cults that exist in North America today is difficult to pinpoint. The American Family Foundation, another national cult-watching group believes that there are more than 2,000 cults in North America and that half of those are damaging. Other estimates by cult experts range from 500 to 5,000.

Most damaging cults are made up of only a handful of members and are relatively invisible. A few cults claim thousands of adherents and collect millions of dollars in fund-raising efforts. The range of cult beliefs is a wide one. Some groups declare themselves satanists and maintain that they dabble in the black arts, but others subscribe to Christian beliefs quite similar to those held by millions. Yet others are led by spiritual teachers who allege to be psychics or healers. Some are formed around leaders who say that they are enlightened and who have moved to the United States from other parts of the world, such as the Far East and the Middle East, often relocating because they couldn't gain followers in their own countries.

Although most groups considered cults today center around religious ideas and teachers, not all of them do. Lyndon LaRouche founded an extremely conservative presidential campaign organization. Currently he is serving a fifteen-year sentence in a Minnesota prison for mail fraud, conspiracy, and failure to pay his taxes. Even so, his followers continue to believe that LaRouche alone can solve the problems of the United States, so they continue to give his organization their life savings. In 1990, federal agents seized documents from the organization's West Virginia headquarters that showed LaRouche had talked elderly people out of tens of millions of dollars to ensure the political salvation of the United States and themselves along with it.

Political organizations, self-improvement seminars, therapy groups, and drug treatment groups may form around a leader whom members believe has special access to the truth. When believers look upon a leader like LaRouche as their only salvation from problems like unhappiness, unemployment, or crime, their devotion becomes the entire focus of their lives. For these people, political or psychological beliefs take on the intensity of religious beliefs. They are easily manipulated by a leader who is out to take advantage of them.

2

Cults Then and Now

His followers isolated themselves from the world, living in a school their spiritual leader had established. Geometry was their main subject—he taught that mathematics would provide them with all the answers about God, whom he called the One. He also believed in past lives. Strict vegetarians, the students tried to abstain from all pleasures, certain that if they lived pure lives their souls would become godlike. They adored their spiritual teacher, believing he had magical or superhuman powers. People claimed that he could appear in two places at once. He was also believed to have performed many other miracles, including taming wild animals by whispering in their ears.

Cults are nothing new. They have existed throughout the world as long as history has been recorded. The religious group described above has many similarities to the cults described in the previous chapter, yet it was founded well over 2,000 years ago by Pythagoras, who is today sometimes called the father of geometry.

Damaging groups tend to increase in number during times of religious fervor or the excitement that comes in the wake of major changes like war, famine, disease, and the introduction of new technology. As people try to find reasons for what is happening and adjust to new ways of living, they turn to religion for answers. When old ways of believing don't seem to offer help, new religions are formed. Some of these, like the group founded by Pythagoras, are cults. In Europe during the Middle Ages and the Renaissance, alchemists gathered cults of followers as they searched for the formula that would turn lead to gold. Before the Russian Revolution in 1917, many people desperately clung to spiritual teachers to help them find inner calm. Rasputin, called the mad monk, was one of those teachers.

A Breeding Ground for Cults

Because it has offered refuge to people persecuted for their religious beliefs, North America has always been an especially fertile breeding ground for cults and cult-like groups. The Puritans fled Europe and settled in New England because the way they worshipped and lived was not accepted by their neighbors. Although the Puritans and the groups that followed, including the Society of Friends, or Quakers, weren't cults, they established a tradition of religious experimentation that others followed. Some of the cults that arose are now forgotten. They attracted few adherents and died with their leader.

Jemima Wilkinson was born to a Quaker family in Rhode Island in 1752. By the time she was twenty, she had memorized most of the Bible. That year she became sick with a fever. Her family, believing that their daughter had died, washed and dressed her for burial. As her funeral procession was leaving the house, Jemima Wilkinson sat up. Those who saw her believed she had come back to life. She told them that she had been picked by God to start a church whose members would not have sexual relations and who would ascend to heaven when Christ came to earth for a second time in 1786. She attracted a number of followers who called her "The Universal Friend" and believed she could interpret dreams and heal the sick. They believed she had come to save the world and stayed loyal even when the world didn't end in 1786.

A master manipulator, Jemima Wilkinson once told her flock to follow her to the edge of a lake where she said she could walk across the water as Christ had. When they had gathered there, she asked them if they believed in her. After they all said yes, she turned back. Secure in their faith, she had no need to perform the miracle. Before she died in 1820, she told her followers not to bury her because she would rise from the dead again. After hiding her body, they waited. When it was clear that she would not come to life, one by one they left, disillusioned.

Several cults begun during the 1800s became very wealthy and attracted a large number of followers. In many ways they resembled the mega-cults of today like the Unification Church and Scientology. One of these early groups was the community of Harmony established by George Rapp, a German who came to America in 1803. Even as a child, Rapp had preached sermons. By the time he was thirty, he was still preaching, and had been taken to court by the Lutherans for stealing members from their congregations. Sixteen years later, George Rapp's speaking abilities had helped him acquire 12,000 followers throughout Germany. Fleeing persecution from the Lutherans, over 500 Rappites, as they were called, moved to the United States where they bought land in Pennsylvania.

During the first year, the group cleared 150 acres and built a church and some cabins. Within five years they had planted 2,000 acres as well as constructing 130 buildings to house their members who now numbered 700. The main reason for this rapid progress was that in 1807 Rapp had forbidden sexual relations between all members—even married couples. There were to be no more children. Every bit of his followers' energy must go into the work of building the community. Those who stayed and added to their families were treated harshly.

When Rapp's only son died in 1812, neighbors claimed that he died because Rapp had castrated him. They were also jealous of the group's wealth. The community of Harmony had become so rich that it caused Rapp problems in other ways. Because his followers no longer had to work so hard, they had time to question their leader's total control over their lives.

Trouble with his neighbors and his need for control caused Rapp to begin a new community in Indiana. When the second community flourished, George Rapp resorted to new methods to keep his followers in line. He told them that he had personally talked to the angel Gabriel. As proof he pointed to a set of bare footprints on a limestone slab he had brought from St. Louis and set at the edge of the Mississippi River.

Ten years later Rapp decided to return his flock to Pennsylvania where he established another settlement, called Economy. By 1826 there were 1,000 Economites, working at community-owned factories four stories tall. The bubble burst when charismatic Rapp died in 1840. Without his leadership, the community began to falter and thirty years later only 100 people remained at Economy.

A Religious Revival

A number of new religions began to spring up during the middle of the 1800s, a time when circuit riding preachers crisscrossed every bit of the frontier to hold revivals. Cut off from family and friends, settlers in these regions took comfort at these gatherings. So many revival meetings were held in New York west of the Catskill and Adirondack mountains that preachers called it the "burned-over district"—there was no unsaved soul left to convert. When the

Erie Canal was finished in 1825, a new wave of people flooded the area. Then came the Panic of 1837, the worst depression the country had seen. Out of this turmoil sprang several cults.

John Humphrey Noyes had been converted at a revival in his hometown of Putney, Vermont, in 1831. He believed that if his intentions were good then anything he did was fine with God, even if it was against the law. The law that bothered Noyes most was that of marriage. Noyes gathered followers by preaching that free love, or "complex marriage," was what God wanted.

In 1846 he put his notions into practice. First he made an agreement between his wife, himself, and another couple that allowed them to switch mates. Slowly Noyes widened the circle to include others, and finally he did away with separate households and private ownership of property.

Noyes' followers were told to keep their sleeping arrangements secret, but two men in the group, angered that three young girls had been included in the group marriage, reported what was going on to the authorities. A grand jury indicted Noyes on two counts of adultery. Rather than stand trial, he moved to the "burned-out" district of New York State and started a community called Oneida where his followers could do as they believed.

At Oneida, Noyes began dictating his followers sexual lives in order to establish paradise on earth. Teenagers as young as thirteen were sexually initiated by older members of the opposite sex. At the same time members were told to change sleeping partners, they were ordered not to form emotional attachments with them. If a couple at Oneida fell in love, they were banned from sleeping with each other. In time, members who had sex were forbidden from spending the night together because they might talk and grow to care about each other.

Though Noyes preached that happiness was part of becoming perfect, he had no sense of humor and, like many modern cult leaders, demanded total obedience from his followers. When he wanted more children at Oneida, Noyes and his assistants carefully matched men and women in order to produce the most beautiful and intelligent children possible. Because Noyes considered himself perfect, he fathered ten children. His male followers, less perfect, were allowed to father only one or two. Slowly the community grew with members supporting themselves by making and selling animal traps and traveling bags.

When Noyes grew old, he seemed bored with his experiment. A son, who had succeeded him to leadership, wasn't charismatic. The children born to selected couples now were teenagers. They began to question their parents lives, so different from those of neighbors. They wanted to fall in love and have families. The surrounding community was up in arms, too, threatening statutory rape charges. Noyes escaped across the Canadian border on June 22, 1879. Another son turned Oneida into a business community engaged in making and selling silverware. Although the cult is no more, the company still exists today.

Other experiences in communal living in addition to those of Rapp and Noyes flourished during the middle of the 1800s. The Shakers in New York State, the members of Amana in Iowa and Brook Farm in Massachusetts all lived apart from the world and were devoted to visionary leaders who claimed their inspiration to start these communes came directly from God.

From Cult to Religion

Two of the groups founded at this time gathered to wait for the second coming of Christ, which they were certain would happen at any moment. Both have worked their way from early cult beginnings to established religions in American culture today.

The Seventh-Day Adventists were begun by William Miller who announced that Christ would reappear on earth between March 21, 1843, and March 21, 1844. At that time believers would be taken up to heaven, he said. Many of Miller's followers even ordered ascension robes to wear when they met their Maker, and they gathered to wait for the grand event. When March 21, 1844, passed and Christ had not appeared, Miller told his flock he had been wrong. Many of them were certain that he had only made a mistake in math and began telling others that the world would end on October 22.

Again nothing happened. Many dropped out. Those who remained faithful called that time the Great Disappointment. (Years later David Koresh's Branch Davidians, a splinter group of the Adventist church, would endure a similar experience and name it the Great Disappointment, too.)

One of the Adventists who stayed was a farmer named Hiram Edson. Walking through a cornfield, he had a vision that the cleansing Miller had predicted was heavenly rather than on the earth where followers could observe it. Christ wouldn't actually return to earth until believers got rid of their sins. Miller and his mentor, Ellen G. White, taught that cutting down the amount of meat they ate and celebrating the Sabbath on Saturday were the best ways to begin. In 1855 Miller and White moved the Seventh-Day Adventists to Battle Creek, Michigan. It was there that one of White's students invented a vegetarian diet of processed corn. His name was Dr. John H. Kellogg. Many people still eat Dr. Kellogg's corn flakes, unaware of their cult beginnings.

The Church of Jesus Christ of Latter Day Saints, or Mormon church, was begun by Joseph Smith Jr. in western New York State. In a vision, Jesus Christ told him not to join an established church because all churches were wrong. Later Smith had another vision in which an angel named Moroni told him that the story of the first North Americans was engraved on some plates buried nearby.

Smith claimed to have found the plates and in 1830 published his translation, the *Book of Mormon*. More visions led him to start his own church on that year. He soon attracted a congregation, and they moved to Kirkland, Ohio, where they build a temple. Smith ruled the group with an iron hand, continuing to have revelations, which he wrote down in a book called *The Doctrines and Covenants*.

Eight years later they moved to Missouri and the next year to Nauvoo, Illinois, turning it into the largest city in the state. From Nauvoo, Smith sent his first missionaries to Europe and told members of yet another revelation he'd had—that God wanted him to have more than one wife. (Before Smith died, he was rumored to have married between 27 and 84 wives.)

Soon after his vision, Smith's many wives caused trouble among his followers. He responded with another revelation that directed church elders to take multiple wives. Some of them started a newspaper to challenge Smith and his ideas. He ordered the newspaper office destroyed and, as a result, was thrown in jail with his brother. While he was in jail, an angry mob broke in, killing both Joseph Smith and his brother.

Brigham Young, an elder in the church who had eighteen wives, took over leadership. In 1848 Young ordered the cross-country trek of the Mormons to Utah. There, in 1852, he announced that God wanted *all* male believers to have more than one wife. To underscore his teaching, he took nine more wives. The U.S. governent responded to the doctrine of the Church of Jesus Christ of Latter Day Saints by passing the Edmunds Bill, which took away the voting rights of all polygamists. Shortly after the passage of the bill, the church changed its teachings to forbid multiple marriages.

During the lifetimes of Joseph Smith and Brigham Young the Church of Jesus Christ of Latter Day Saints had the traits of a cult, but over the last century it has grown to be a major denomination that now claims almost three million members throughout North America and the rest of the world.

Things That Go Bump in the Night

Spiritualism, the forerunner of modern channeling, began in New York State in 1848. Two young sisters, Kate and Margaretta Fox, had heard strange knockings in their bedrooms during the first three months that their family had lived in their Hydesville home. On March 31, Kate snapped her fingers a few times and called, "Here, Mr. Splitfoot, do as I do." She heard the same number of raps as finger snappings. The Fox family soon devised a system to communicate with the rapper. They claimed that the noises were made by the spirit of a peddler named Charles Roena, murdered five years earlier in that very house. Next they dug in their basement and told visitors that they had found human bones. Soon afterward the girls moved to Rochester, New York, and the rappings stopped.

Spiritualism didn't. Like wildfire, the idea of talking to the dead caught on across North America as all kinds of spirit entities suddenly began to communicate with the living. Respected clergy and scientists criticized the movement, but it continued to grow. In 1853, one Spiritualist newsletter said 40,000 Spiritualists lived in New York State alone. Mediums who communicated with these spirits traveled throughout the country, giving lectures and demonstrations. A number of publications appeared repeating spirit messages and advising readers how to communicate.

Although Spiritualism was never formally organized as one church, some individual groups, centering around a particular medium, became small cults. Members of these groups would give every bit of money they had, to hear messages channeled through a group leader during a ceremony called a seance. They followed the advice given in these messages without question.

As a trend, Spiritualism began to decline during the late 1850s and early 1860s. The first reason for this loss of interest was the Civil War, which proved a more compelling distraction than chatting with ghosts. The second reason was that those who believed that they really received spirit messages began making attempts to expose fakes who used seances and phoney spirit messages to make money. In 1864 they formed the first national association and others followed. Their clean-up campaign worked so well that soon many people believed that all mediums were frauds.

Spiritualism became popular once more in the 1890s and then during the period between World Wars I and II that saw the Roaring Twenties and the Great Depression. Again it fell into decline, reviving in the 1970s with the publication of Jane Robert's books in which she recorded messages that she claimed to receive from a spirit named Seth.

Today's mediums are usually called *channelers.* The two most popular ones are J. Z. Knight, who claims to share communications from Ramtha, a spirit whom she says was a warrior 5,000 years ago in a life before this one, and Jach Pursel, who claims to channel a spirit named Lazaris. These channelers typically go into trances in front of large audiences. They also make audio- and videotapes of these spirit appearances. Some channelers charge high fees for individual counseling sessions.

The God of Harlem

Between the First and Second World Wars, many African Americans moved from the rural South to cities in the North in order to find work. Big city life was a difficult adjustment for some to make. George Baker, later known as Father Divine, took advantage of the migrants' dislocation from home and family.

Born in Georgia in the late 1800s, George Baker served as a part-time Baptist preacher in Baltimore whe he was twenty years old. Later he moved to Brooklyn where he lived with between thirty and forty followers, forming a group called the Peace Movement. He told his followers that Heaven was here on earth. Sickness, death, and sin were signs of lack of faith. If followers believed in their Father, their every need would be taken care of. From 1919 to 1931, he began gathering more followers around him, including whites, by offering free chicken dinners, inexpensive shelter, and an employment agency—powerful attractions during the middle of the Great Depression. In the meantime, Father Divine moved to Harlem and began teaching that he was God.

In 1931 the police arrested him because the crowds who attended his church, eager to witness his healing abilities, had caused a traffic jam. Against the advice of the jury, the judge sentenced the god of Harlem to a year in jail. Two days later the judge was dead of a heart attack. Father Divine responded by saying to followers, "I hated to do it!" Soon afterward, his conviction was overturned.

For years Divine's loyal following celebrated the day the judge had died as a church holiday. Father Divine married a Canadian woman, Edna Ritchings, in 1946, and she became known as Mother Divine. They moved from Harlem to a house in Philadelphia, a gift from a follower. At his death in 1965, his home became a shrine. The Peace Movement still exists, but membership has dwindled dramatically.

Spiritual Rebels

The next great surge in North American cult activity occurred during the 1960s, a time of riots, civil rights conflicts, and the Vietnam War. President John F. Kennedy was assassinated, as were Martin Luther King, Jr., Robert

Kennedy, and Malcolm X. As the post–World War II baby boomers became teenagers in the 1960s, they considered themselves very special people, probably because there were so many of them. They also believed they were very different from their parents—they were rebels *with* a cause, out to change the world. Many rejected the mainstream religious beliefs of their families, turning instead toward religions that had come from other parts of the world, Neopaganism, and strict, Bible-based Christian groups. Many of these organizations were cults. While some have faded, others remain strong today.

The list of all the cults born in the 1960s is too long to give here. Some of them, like Scientology, the Unification Church, and Synanon are discussed elsewhere. Other significant cults of the 1960s are detailed below:

Hare Krishna: The International Society for Krishna Consciousness

Begun in the United States in 1965, the International Society for Krishna Consciousness, ISKCON, is a group that follows a new interpretation of the teachings of a 16th-century Bengali saint. Its founder A. C. Bhaktivedanta Swami Prabhupada, moved to North America when he was 70 after a vision told him to become a missionary to the West. His efforts attracted huge numbers of white, middle-class teenagers. Today there are 43 large Hare Krishna temples in the United States as well as six farms and thirteen restaurants, but the group attracts more Indian converts, while the number of non-Indian members shrinks.

The religious practices the leader taught before his death in 1977 included chanting the names of God, or Krishna, over and over again to achieve a state of bliss. Hare Krishnas take a new name when they join, and many men shave their head. Members dress like religious students in India and spend much of their time chanting and selling the group's publications on street corners to raise funds.

Although the Krishnas believe in nonviolence, leaders have admitted to arming their farm communes. New Vrindaban, the farm commune that is headquarters for ISKCON of West Virginia, faced a federal investigation that resulted in the 1991 conviction of leaders for arson, conspiracy, and racketeering. One leader was convicted in a murder trial for the shooting death of a former resident of the commune.

Neopaganism or Wicca

Like Spiritualism, Neopaganism and Wicca, or Witchcraft, are not large organized groups. Neopaganism is a broad term for what believers call *Earth-based religions* or *shamanism*—pre-Christian spiritual practices. Wicca, sometimes called the *Old Religion,* is based on European pre-Christian traditions. The movement consists of small groups of believers. In Wicca the groups are called *covens.* While the entire movement is by no means a cult, covens and Neopagan groups *can* be mini-cults if they are led by an authoritarian high priest or priestess or a power-hungry person claiming to be a shaman.

Most people who say they believe in Wicca and practice witchcraft today study the works of Gerald Gardner or Alexander Sanders, two 20th-century authors who claimed to have special knowledge of old beliefs and ceremonies. Those who follow Gardner are called Gardnerarians, and those who follow Sanders are termed Alexandrians.

Most of the 40,000 witches and Neopagans in North America today worship the Goddess and her mate, the Horned God. (Feminist covens worship only the Goddess.) During the Middle Ages, the Catholic church mislabeled the image of the male god worshipped by those it wished to convert as the devil talked about in the Bible. Since that time witches have often been falsely accused of devil worshipping or satanism, something far from the truth. While most Neopagans claim to believe in magic and practice it, their ethics direct them to use spells for healing rather than harm. They teach that any harm done will come back three times over to the person who has cast the spell.

Children of God

Originally called the Family of Love, this group was founded on the West Coast by David Berg in the late 1960s when he preached a Jesus revolution (a combination of Bible teachings and 1960s social change and protest) to teenage street people who had flocked to California during that time. In 1968 he had a vision that an earthquake was coming, so he and his group moved to Arizona. There some fifty members split into four missionary teams. Berg accompanied one of the teams to Montreal where he had more revelations and officially began his organization. Soon afterward came the name Children of God.

Dressed in red sack cloth, decorated in ashes, and practicing communal sex, Berg's children grew in number. In part, their numbers increased due to a recruiting practice Berg invented for female members called "flirty fishing," or becoming prostitutes for Jesus. Soon Berg was sending members out to establish forty new colonies. His sacred texts were the *Mo Letters,* which detailed his conversations with a spirit called Abrahim, a gypsy king. (Mo stood for Moses, the name Berg's followers used for him.)

At its peak, the Children of God claimed their membership was close to a million. By the 1980s, after the mass suicides at Jonestown had caused people to seriously question Christian cults, few traces of the group remained in North America. Several hundred Children of God still possibly exist, but the group has no North American centers, and the headquarters has been moved to London.

Cults for the 1990s

Many of the cults that blossomed during the stormy 1960s and into the 1970s, grew very slowly or declined over the decade of the 1980s. Currently, cults are on the rise once again as family violence, high crime rates, and a troubled economy have young people once again looking for answers. The current generation of cults differs some from those that have come before. Except for the highly organized Bible-based cults, today's damaging religious groups tend to be smaller, consisting of a handful of followers organized around a teacher or leader.

New Age Groups

Some of these teachers claim to be part of the New Age movement, a loose set of spiritual ideas that combines Far Eastern religion and Western mystical ideas. Recently they have begun to mix Native American traditions into their teachings. New Agers believe in developing their psychic potential, in healing themselves and the planet, and in creating the New Age, a form of heaven on Earth. They follow many different spiritual traditions and practices, including meditating with crystals, channeling, astrology, psychic readings, and hypnosis to explore past lives that many say they have experienced.

From time to time a New Age *guru,* or teacher, takes advantage of the anything-goes nature of New Age beliefs and makes major headlines. Police in New York City are convinced that Frederick von Mierers, who was found dead of AIDS-related pneumonia in 1990, robbed people of millions of dollars by selling them worthless gemstones for outrageously high prices. Von Mierers, who claimed that he was from another galaxy and had come to fight dark forces on this planet, founded a New York City cult called Eternal Values. He taught Eastern religion and astrology, admired Adolf Hitler, and engaged in group sex. His treatments involved giving clients "life readings" and telling them how to heal themselves by wearing certain gems, which he conveniently sold at a huge mark-up. Among the taken were top models, actors, and actresses.

Marshall Applewhite joined thirty-nine of his followers in a mass suicide that took place in their Rancho Santa Fe, California home. The cult members, high-tech New Agers who earned money by designing Internet Web pages, suffocated themselves to death by placing plastic bags over their heads after drinking vodka mixed with barbiturates in March 1997. Material that the Heaven's Gate cult members posted on their own Web pages led investigators to conclude that they believed the appearance of the Hale-Bopp comet was a signal to them that they should depart for another world.

Satanism

While New Age teachers generally claim to fight dark forces, leaders of satanic groups worship these forces. The church of Satan, which was founded in 1966 by Anton La Vey, had never managed to gain more than between 250 and 500 followers over the next twenty years, even though La Vey wrote books on devil worship, including *The Satanic Bible,* and often appeared on television. The next largest satanic organization in North America had only twenty-five members.

Then in 1980, a book called *Michelle Remembers* was published. In it the author told of her experiences under hypnosis, which led her to remember ritual satanic abuse. Smith claimed that her parents had been members of a Vancouver satanic group and that, as a child, she had been tortured and raped. At the same time as Michelle Smith's book came out, conservative Christian groups were accusing contemporary rock bands of being devil worshippers and promoting satanism.

Suddenly a number of women started coming forward, saying that they had experienced similar abuse at the hands of Satanists and had only recently remembered it. They detailed stories of human sacrifices and of young virgins being made pregnant. Next, legal charges of satanic ritual abuse were filed across North America. Some of the abuse was said to have occurred at day-care centers. Whole communities were torn apart, but when these accusations were brought to court, most of them were dismissed for lack of evidence. Sometimes professional investigators were shown to have placed ideas into witnesses' minds and words into their mouths that supported the strange accusations. In the meantime, hurt by the bad publicity, Anton La Vey disbanded the active chapters of his organization, and although he continued to accept individual members, today he communicates with them only by mail.

As the stories continued to mount during the 1980s, the total of alleged sacrifices was well into the thousands and the number of Satanic groups that ritual abuse survivors claimed existed in the 1960s and 1970s was in the hundreds. When no bodies or other evidence was found to support these stories, the psychological community began to suspect that mass hysteria like that during the Salem Witch Trials in 1692, rather than satanism, was at work. Although they do not deny that some teenagers and adults dabble in satanism in groups, most mental health experts believe that the damage these groups do is emotional, not physical or supernatural. While anticult and conservative Christian groups continue to fight a war against the cult of Satanism, the American Psychiatric Association released a position statement in 1994, which cast doubts on the accuracy of repressed memories such as those described by ritual abuse survivors.

Christian Groups

On the opposite end of the spectrum from Satanic groups are the Biblical Shepherding, Discipleship or Multiplying Ministry movements, like the Boston Church of Christ, which have grown rapidly during the past decade. The Boston Church of Christ is *not* connected to the larger Church of Christ denomination, which heatedly criticizes the group. It *is* scattered throughout North America. Founded in Boston by evangelist Kip McKean in 1979, the group boasted thirty members. Today weekly services in Boston draw more than 2,000 worshippers. When the collection plate is passed at these services, sometimes the amount donated is over $35,000.

The goal of the Boston Church of Christ and other Multiplying Ministries is to save as many people in as short a time as possible. Once a person has converted to the group's idea of Christianity, he or she must immediately win new members, using any way that works—even lying. In the meantime, members are often ordered to give up family, school, or work in order to save souls on a full-time basis. Soon afterward, they become disciplers or shepherds and are put in charge of newer members, making sure that they have no free time in which to question their conversion, the group, or its leaders. Even though these groups may teach beliefs very similar to those preached in Sunday sermons throughout North America, their actions, especially the methods they use to gain new members, can be very harmful.

Hate Groups

During the last decade, a number of neo-Nazi hate groups have arisen that teach a combination of religion and racism. The three organizations that monitor these organized hate groups estimate that they have from 10,000 to 20,000 members and ten times as many supporters.

Patterned loosely after the Nazi Party and the Ku Klux Klan, these organizations preach *anti-Semitism* (hatred of Jews) and that the white race is superior to all other races, and leaders often misinterpret passages from the Bible in order to back up their point. One of these groups, the Christian Identity Movement, believes that Jews are descended from the devil and that God's chosen people in the Bible are all white Anglo-Saxons. They also teach that all people of color were put on Earth before Adam so they aren't human, but a lower species. Other targets of these groups' wrath are gays.

Most organized hate groups have rigid rules and power structures. Leaders of many hate groups exert a great deal of control over their members' lives, telling them where to live and with whom they can associate. Some groups encourage their members to shave their heads, to wear uniforms, and to cut off contact with their families if they don't share the new member's racist beliefs. Some of these organizations stockpile weapons and hold military training exercises in preparation for a race war.

Some of these neo-Nazi groups urge their members toward violence in order to get rid of people who oppose their beliefs and to form a racially "pure" society. The Church of the Creator, a Los Angeles–based racist organization, plotted to bomb a black church in order to kill black leaders. In Portland, Oregon, three members of the Aryan Youth Movement, a part of the White Aryan Resistance, killed an Ethiopian man. The legal system held the group's national leader, John Metzger, and his son, the head of the Aryan Youth Movement, responsible for inciting the hate crime because of their teachings, even though they had never personally met the killers. A jury ordered a $12.5 million judgment against the two.

These racist groups recruit new members in prisons and among teenagers, especially those adolescents who call themselves skinheads. The skinhead movement began a decade ago as a reaction to punk music and punk rockers. Although it started out as a way of dressing and listening to a certain style of music, over the past years, skinheads have been growing more political. Not all skinheads are racist, but according to the Anti-Defamation League of the B'nai B'rith, there are 3,500 racist skinheads in the United States today.

Are hate groups cults? Based on what you know from your reading so far, you decide?

3

Who Joins Cults?

Although Tina is in ninth grade, her mom is so protective that she's still choosing Tina's clothes to make sure they aren't "too revealing." Life has gotten even worse now that Tina's father has left. Her mother now insists that Tina not date, and Tina knows her mom snoops in her room to look for hints of a secret boyfriend. Even her older brother follows her around and spies on her after school. She hates the way they treat her. It isn't Tina's fault that her mother is so angry at Tina's dad that she hates all men. It isn't Tina's fault that her older sister became pregnant, dropped out of school, and ran away from home. Tina isn't her sister—she's *herself*. Why can't anybody in her family see that? Lately, she's been wishing she could do something, anything, just to make them all shut up and leave her alone.

Every morning Jamal walks to school past new gang graffiti, spray-painted on buildings overnight. The house a block from where he lives is now a crack house. Even though there have been no drive-by shootings on his street yet, several have occurred throughout the neighborhood. A friend's older brother died in one of them. Things have really changed since elementary school when neighbors gathered in backyards for barbecues, and little kids rode their bikes up and down the sidewalk until late on summer nights. Now everybody lives in fear.

Jamal doesn't want to join a gang, but his friends say it is the only way to survive—gang members *protect* family and friends from violence. This is war, and there is safety in numbers, they tell him. Maybe they are right. He isn't sure anymore.

When Frank met Judy at a teen dance club, he felt something special for her right away. They liked the same music, movies, and food. Their friends thought they were the perfect couple. His parents were especially pleased that their son was dating a girl who went to Mass regularly. Maybe Judy would make him settle down and get better grades instead of spending hours banging on his drums and tinkering with cars.

When Judy began attending psychological self-improvement classes at the home of a girl she'd met at school, Frank thought it was fine as long as she didn't pressure him to improve. After meeting Judy's new friend, he wasn't so sure. She had a blank smile on her face even when she started talking about preparing for the end of the world, and she did a lot of talking about that. Frank still couldn't figure out what the end of the world had to do with self-improvement. Then Judy began bugging him to come to the class with her just once. He didn't want to go, but it was obviously important to her. He supposed he'd give it a shot. One boring evening couldn't hurt, could it?

Tina, Jamal, and Frank are all fairly typical teenagers. They also have one other thing in common—they are all prime candidates for cult recruiters.

"How could that be," you might be thinking, "people who join cults are either crazy or stupid. They're life's losers, aren't they?" Wrong! That's a comforting myth most damaging cult leaders would very much like all teenagers to believe. People who fall for it are overly confident when cult recruiters approach. Throwing caution to the wind, they become prime candidates for cult membership.

In reality, damaging cults want bright, energetic, and relatively well-adjusted people who can give money, time, and talents to help further the group's goals. In fact, several studies show that people who are approached and eventually join cults tend to be of average or above average intelligence. Many are well-educated. Few could be called crazy. In fact, cult researcher Dr. Margaret Singer believes that at least three-quarters of all cult members are "basically normal."

According to research conducted by psychologist George Swope, who interviewed 125 former cult members, many people join cults out of simple curiosity, while others are trying to find their identity. Some of them, like Tina, may be tempted to join in order rebel and to gain independence from problem families. Potential cult members also tend to be idealistic. Others, like Jamal, are frustrated at the way the world is. Still others join because they want to know God better. They seek meaning and purpose as well as answers to their spiritual questions. Some people join cults because they care very deeply for a person involved with a damaging cult. Like Frank, they may be pulled into the group to keep that relationship intact.

Teens and Cults

Simply being a teenager can make you a cult target because adolescence is a *life transition,* a time of many changes when suddenly the old rules don't work. The journey from childhood to adulthood can be a bumpy ride as teens learn to get along with their families while gaining independence from them. At the same time adolescents try to avoid being pushed around by friends, they must work hard to fit in with the crowd. The major physical changes adolescents face certainly don't make life any easier.

During transitions like these, we are forced to give up our old ways and to live "on empty" for a while before we find the new methods of coping that will work for us. It takes even longer before we're familiar and comfortable with who we've become after making these changes. According to the psychologists who study cults, we are most vulnerable to believing what cult recruiters tell us when we:

- feel like we need to find some answers, and we need to find them fast,
- have our confidence shaken by crisis,
- aren't quite sure about how we should act,
- find ourselves in vague or confusing situations,
- are uncertain about our own beliefs and values.

Many teenagers aren't sure about what they want or who they are. Something that will cause them to feel happy one minute will be boring, unpleasant, or frustrating the next. Their feelings race around with amazing speed. Other teens are filled with questions and desperate for answers. When they're told they must come up with their *own* answers, it can feel like being dumped right in the middle of a very large lake and not knowing how to swim to the shore. They may thrash for a while and feel out of control, like they are drowning. Even when they figure out how to keep afloat, they may swim back and forth several times until they get their bearings.

Adolescents can face other stressful transitions that leave them feeling vulnerable and confused about life and themselves. Some of those transitions are:

- breaking-up with a boyfriend or girlfriend,
- coping with parents' divorce,
- adjusting to a friend's or family member's death,
- moving to another state, city, or neighborhood,

- changing schools,
- living away from home for the first time.

It is no wonder that cult recruiters often focus their efforts on teenagers. According to reports by cult monitoring groups, such as the Cult Awareness Network and the American Family Foundation, a number of cult members join when they are as young as sixteen. About half of all current cult members are eighteen to twenty-five years old. Cult recruiters know that the teen years are a time of seeking direction, and they are more than willing to point the way—right into a damaging cult. Some recruiters make a special effort to contact potential teenage members during times of stress, such as final exam week or graduation, when they will be more vulnerable.

Even though many adolescents without jobs may not be able to bring money into the group, they are valuable to cults because they have many talents and a great deal of energy. Since young people have an easy time building rapport and gaining the trust of other young people, teenagers make good recruiters. Dangerous cults can also put them to work building the community or fund-raising. Finally, some damaging cults seek out young members because they hope these recruits will marry other cult members and will later give their children to the cult.

Adults at Risk

Teenagers can be hurt by cults without ever joining them if their parents belong to damaging organizations. Like Audrey, they may feel resentful when a parent spends money on cult activities that they feel should go toward meeting their family's needs. Adult cult members often have little time for being a parent. Some simply ignore their children, and others actually abandon their families to move to a cult's group house. Teenage children are forced into the role of adult, taking care of themselves while fearing for a parent's safety and well-being. They may feel helpless because they can do little or nothing to convince Mom or Dad to break with the dangerous group.

Adults face many transitions in their lives that make them targets for cult recruiters. When someone loses a long-held job, that person questions his or her self-worth. The unemployed adult may feel like he or she has no purpose in life, that nothing makes sense any more. He or she may go through a period of self-definition much like that of adolescence. Divorce can have the same impact on a person. Many adults go through something called *mid-life crisis* as they make the transition from being a younger adult to becoming an older one. As adults reach mid-life (40 to 60 years of age), their bodies start to show signs of age. Since our culture places such a high emphasis on being young and attractive, it's a rare person who greets gray hair and wrinkles cheerfully. This is a time of life when both men and women begin to reflect on how they've spent their years so far and, because they know they aren't going to live forever, what they want to do with the rest of their lives. After *menopause,* or change of life, women are no longer able to have children. Some of them have a difficult time adjusting to the physical changes their bodies are going through and to the new way of looking at themselves. When children grow up and start leaving home, parents must adjust to their new-found freedom. They may ask themselves the same questions as teenagers in the middle of an identity crisis: "Who am I?" and "What do I do with my life now?"

Observers of damaging cults have noticed that cult recruiters are turning their attention to people, especially women, facing mid-life crisis. Currently membership in many psychotherapy, self-help, and New Age cults is composed mainly of women in their forties and fifties. Often these women have jobs or are married to men who work. They have money to spend on seminars, tapes, and other cult materials, and they are looking for some meaning in life beyond the role of mom or wife. Even grandparents aren't safe from cult recruiters. Senior citizens, who have worked all their lives and have now retired, are very attractive to cults. Frequently older people have saved money for their retirement for most of their lives, money that damaging-cult leaders would love to get their hands on. These people may also be facing illness, the death of a spouse, or trying to work through fear of their own death. Like adolescents and people going through a mid-life crisis, they, too, are forced to make changes in their self-identity and must redefine who they are and what they want out of life.

Since our society is a mobile one, extended families are often scattered across the country. Adult children may not be there to help older parents as they were several generations ago. In addition, many older Americans retire to the Sun Belt, the part of the United States with the mildest winters, often removing themselves from their support network of friends and family. The loneliness they can feel when they make these changes can cause them to trust cult recruiters.

Professional cult observers have tracked a growing interest in senior citizens among damaging cults. Some cults even hide their recruiting pitches beneath recreational outings or self-improvement seminars at senior citizen centers. Recruiters are also starting to focus their efforts on retirement communities and nursing homes, offering companionship and attention in the hope that older people will join the cult, change their wills, and then die, leaving all their money to the organization. The Unification Church has established the Orange Blossom Corps, a group of recruiters who target senior citizens.

From Damaging Family to Damaging Cult

People facing mid-life crisis, those people who have recently moved, and senior citizens aren't the only ones whose loneliness makes them hungry for the feeling of belonging that cults can provide. Anyone who has grown up in what psychologists call a *dysfunctional family,* one that fails to meet the needs of its members for nurturing and support, may long to know what it is like to live in a good family with caring parents.

Bonita's mom is an active alcoholic who claims to love her daughter but spends most evenings lying on the living room sofa, a bottle of wine nearby. Bonita has no one to turn to when she needs advice—her mom is often passed out. She would talk to her dad, but he's too busy, and the only thing he thinks about is how to get his wife to stop drinking. Nobody even notices when Bonita sneaks out to spend the night with friends. Often it seems like nobody cares.

Nobody seems to notice, either, that it is Bonita who cooks the meals, does the grocery shopping, cleans the house, and watches her younger brothers. It is Bonita who must listen to her mother's tearful tantrums about how marriage and children have ruined her life and driven her to drink. Forced into assuming the role of an adult, this teenager isn't allowed to be herself.

Alcoholism is only one of the problems that can create a dysfunctional family. Domestic violence between husband and wife, physical or emotional child abuse, and incest can all twist family relationships into unhealthy patterns. Family members spend their lives trying hide the problem from themselves and trying to look good to those outside the family. Counselors call this way of behaving *denial.*

Teenagers who grow up in dysfunctional families tend to have low self-esteem. If a parent verbally abused you, ignored you because he or she was too busy getting drunk or high on drugs, beat you or sexually molested you, you'd probably spend a great deal of time searching for an answer to why things were so bad at home. Even though your parent treated you badly, you'd still depend on that person to put a roof over your head, clothes on your back, and food on the table. If you were like most kids from dysfunctional families, you'd blame *yourself* for what was happening. You'd tell yourself your parent treated you the way he or she did because you were a bad person and you deserved that treatment. Chances are, you'd be ashamed of yourself, and you'd probably get caught up in trying to be a better person in order to get your problem parent to treat you better. When parents don't help their children meet their self-esteem needs, children blame themselves for family problems and don't learn how to feel good about themselves. Instead of feeling okay from the inside out, they to look for self-worth outside themselves. Some kids depend almost entirely on friends to make them happy. Others rely on praise from teachers. They work full time at achieving in schoolwork or sports. Yet others join cults. According to a 1982 study reported by the Committee on Psychiatry and Religion, more than half of the cult members interviewed had come from "mildly to seriously disturbed" families.

By the time Bonita was approached by some teenagers outside her school and invited to begin going to Biblestudy classes for girls, she was more than ready for the attention they gave her. It felt good to be wanted and to feel important. The woman who taught the classes seemed more motherly than Bonita's own mom could ever hope to be. The special interest she showed in Bonita was flattering, and it met a real need in her life—the need to be cared for by an adult who could fill the role of parent. Bonita was so ready for rules instead of the chaos at home that she agreed when the woman told her that jewelry and colorful clothing were sinful and to stop wearing them. Two months into the Bible-study classes, Bonita began spending weekends and whole weeks at the woman's house. It was better than hanging out at home where nobody seemed to care.

Dysfunctional families may be hiding any number of problems, but they all share the same "rules":

- Don't talk about your feelings.
- Don't feel your feelings.
- Don't trust anybody outside the family.

These family rules are very similar to the ones cult members live by. Because distorting the truth is an everyday part of life in a dysfunctional family, teenagers who grow up in families like these usually aren't terribly upset when they discover that cult recruiters and leaders have lied to them. In fact, some can be so good at living by the rules of secrecy and denial that they feel right at home in the dysfunctional family of a damaging cult.

A Search for Spiritual Meaning

We live in a world filled with injustice and violence. By the time they graduate, one in five teenagers will have been threatened with a weapon or injured by one at school, indicates a University of Michigan study. Forty-two percent of all youths aged nine through seventeen fear that some day they might contract the AIDS virus, according to a recent survey conducted by the Yankelovich Youth Monitor. A study done by the National Victim Center reports that well over half a million women were raped in the United States in 1990. Both teenagers and adults have difficulty making sense of these things.

If we're caring people, it hurts us when we turn on the news and see a mother's tears as she grieves the death of her six-year-old daughter killed in a drive-by shooting, her only crime—playing in the front yard at the wrong time. It hurts us when we see the tormented faces of children starving in Somalia, innocent victims of war. We wonder what the world is coming to when a terrorist carries a machine gun into a mosque where people are praying and guns them down or when we hear about the hole in the ozone layer, global warming, the destruction of the rain forest, nuclear waste dumps, and the destruction of Native American sacred sites—often it seems there is no escaping the bad news.

Some of us turn off the TV and stop reading newspapers in an attempt to escape. We tell ourselves that we'll do well in school, focus on our friends and family, and eventually we'll get good jobs and start families of our own. But then we hear that today people with college degrees are having difficulty finding work. Jobs are available, but they are mainly low-skilled and low-paying. Families try to move to neighborhoods that are safe from crime, but they can find no safe neighborhoods. In times of danger and uncertainty, the old rules about how to cope with life simply don't seem to apply.

What does it all mean? Is there a god directing all of this? If there is a god, why does he (or she) let pain and suffering happen? Where do we fit in? Why were we born? Few people can escape asking these questions. We try to sort out the good news from the bad and find explanations, wanting to help straighten out the mess, but what can we do?

When we're actively seeking direction in our lives, cults can be a tempting option because they tell us we don't have to struggle to figure out the meaning of life—*they* have simple answers to all complex questions, if we'll just listen and follow the leader. The moral authority that cults provide is a comfort to many people because it provides the illusion of safety and spares them the work of real learning and decision making. No longer do they have to choose what is right and what is wrong or what actions to take in the confusing situations that happen so frequently today. The cult leader sets it all out in black and white for them. Some people like all the harsh rules a cult insists its members obey, regarding them as a challenge much like advanced algebra or mountain climbing. These people work hard to succeed at getting ahead in the organization.

An aspect of spirituality lacking today in many peoples' lives is a sense of community. Neighbors can live in an apartment building for years and never get to know each other. Parents often move because of job changes so that their children change schools frequently. When that happens, friendships are temporary at best. Cults appear to provide friendship that is permanent. Even better, they also seem at first glance to offer concrete ways to help solve the problems on this earth by working with others. We may feel as though we're participating in something very important and that our lives will become more important if we join the cult.

Many people attend workshops and lectures in order to improve the quality of their life. Some, like Judy are already part of a strong religious tradition. They are accustomed to trusting church leaders, so they don't ask too many questions. These people are often looking for meaning beyond what they have found in Catholicism, Protestantism, or Judaism (the three main religious groups in North America from which cults draw their membership). Others do not have a religious upbringing, and they are unsure of their beliefs. All they know is that they long to believe in something so that their lives will be more fulfilling. Most of the time these attempts at self-improvement by taking classes or belonging to groups are harmless. Some are helpful. Those that involve encounters with damaging cults can be downright dangerous.

When Joanne Sustar, who was forty-two, attended a workshop in North Carolina run by a woman claiming to be a fourth-generation Cherokee medicine woman, all she wanted to do was to explore her spirituality. Nothing about the name of the group sponsoring the workshop, the Center for Human Development, seemed out of the ordinary. In addition to the workshop in which Sustar enrolled, the organization offered classes in dream interpretation and breath therapy as well as spiritual counseling sessions.

When the leader told Sustar to allow a plastic bag to be placed over her head and to be buried under a foot of sand for fifteen minutes, she agreed. After all, she was to be given an air tube to breathe through, and knowing little about Native American spiritual practices, she must have mistakenly assumed this practice was an old one and perfectly safe. Why would a "medicine woman" tell her differently? Sustar didn't question her teacher's training or if she was, in fact, a Native American. She didn't stop to realize that many people try to sell followers phoney ceremonies with no regard for their clients' health or emotional well-being and that this woman was one of them. Minutes later Sustar was dead. She'd inhaled sand, vomited and choked to death on her own vomit.

For Their Own Good

Sometimes well-meaning parents unknowingly place their children in damaging cult settings in order to free them from addiction to alcohol or drugs. The parents have heard that these programs are highly structured and that they have high success rates. Often the drug- or alcohol-abusing teen has "graduated" from several local treatment centers only to relapse. Parents are usually desperate to try anything for a cure when they check their youngsters into drug rehabilitation organizations like Synanon and Straight Inc. or Narconon, which has strong ties to Scientology.

Synanon was founded in the late 1950s by Charles Dederich, himself a recovering alcoholic. He believed that if his patients did hard manual labor and took part in hours-long encounter sessions to break down their defenses and get rid of their harmful personality traits, then they would give up alcohol and drugs. These sessions, which are still held today, are called the "Synanon Game." When clients play this "game," they point out each other's defects, mistakes, and sins. Soon the whole group joins in, yelling profanity and insults. Clients are expected to shave their head and are harshly punished for even the slightest infraction of rules.

At its high point Synanon had 2,000 clients along with 10,000 interested people who only dropped into Synanon treatment centers to play the game. There were centers across the United States and in Malaysia, the Philippines, and West Germany, and the treatment centers were a business worth $20 million. Charismatic Dederich gave countless interviews to newspapers and got a stamp of approval from politicians, ministers, and major corporations. Then he started talking about how the world outside Synanon was evil. Instead of the three-year program it had been, he changed it to a life-long program and removed the graduation. Synanon clients would now stay in treatment until they died. Next Dederich encouraged "lifestylers," non-addicts who wanted to live in Synanon, to do so. They were told to sell all they owned: cars, houses, real estate, and personal possessions, giving the money they made to Synanon. One man signed over more than three-quarters of a million dollars in stock to Dederich.

When Dederich would yell "I can make you insane," at the people who had joined him, they believed him. In 1977, he declared there could be no children in the organization and ordered people to be sterilized. Women were told to abort babies they were then carrying. Many complied. Those who refused couldn't leave gracefully. They were verbally abused, strip searched, and harassed for months afterward by Synanon members who would try to get them fired from the jobs they had managed to get after leaving the group.

Next Dederich ordered a mass-divorce for all the married couples in the group and partner swapping. Two hundred thirty couples filed for divorce. When one couple who had divorced at their leader's orders, became unhappy with their new forced marriages and decided to leave, Dederich was reported to say, "Put those people in a pickup truck and throw them in a ditch."

Today the organization still survives though membership has sharply dropped and lawsuits from former clients have hurt the group financially. In 1990 the Nevada Casino Control Commission barred Synanon and three of its officers from doing business with the gambling casinos in the state after one of the officials was charged with 22 counts of conspiracy to defraud the U.S. government, obstruction of justice, and perjury. The Showboat Hotel Casino had offered Synanon $330,000 to run a motivational seminar for workers. Investigations by law enforcement agencies for terrorism haven't helped the group's popularity either, but unknowing parents still can put their teenagers in Synanon "for their own good."

Straight Inc., which was founded in 1976 and has several treatment centers in various parts of the country, does not have a charismatic leader like Chuck Dederich, but it shares many similar methods of drug treatment. New clients have all their rights taken away and are forbidden to see their families. They are led everywhere, even to the bathroom, by their pant loops. Counseling sessions last as long as ten hours, during which clients can't speak or use the restroom.

Considered a cult by the Cult Awareness Network, the organization has been accused in the courts of sexual, physical, and psychological abuse of clients. In 1985 an 18-year-old woman received a $37,500 court settlement after her claim that she was physically hurt and held against her will in the St. Petersburg, Florida treatment center. In 1990 jurors awarded another former client $721,000.

Against Their Will

Frank plans to attend a cult recruiting seminar at the urging of his girlfriend, Judy. It's difficult to refuse, when someone you like asks you to share something that that person feels is important. It's *especially* difficult to refuse when you have no idea the group is a cult. Even people who aren't married or related to the cult victim, can let their feelings for another blind them to the dangers of involvement with a damaging cult.

Children whose parents join cults often don't have the luxury of saying no to cult membership. Because they depend on their parents to meet their physical needs for survival and because their parents have legal custody to make decisions for them, kids can't refuse to be cult members. They must live, and sometimes die, with the consequences of the choices their parents make.

When William Meyers, a sixteen-year-old, arrived at the North Florida Regional Medical Center in Gainesville, Florida, he weighed 90 pounds, 45 pounds less than he had three months before. Doctors found he was starving to death because a heart tumor that had gone untreated for several months made it difficult for him to keep food in his stomach. Although his parents claimed he'd been walking around until right before he came to the hospital, doctors discovered the teenager had bed sores, which indicated he'd been flat on his back for a long period of time.

William's parents belonged to End Time Ministries, a cult that believes in faith healing. They were arrested and charged with "child abuse: medical neglect." Two weeks before the arrest, they had admitted during a social services hearing to determine their fitness as parents that they were wrong in not getting medical help for their son. William was lucky—he recovered. His baby niece wasn't so fortunate. Only four days old, she had died the year before from internal bleeding caused by a lack of vitamin K, which helps the blood to clot. Chances are high that she would have lived had she been injected with the vitamin, something most hospitals do routinely when infants are first born.

Even when a parent decides to leave a damaging cult, freeing his or her child from the tight grip of that organization can be difficult. Some damaging cults make it a practice to hide the children of cult members when parents leave. This makes it almost impossible for members to walk away. Most refuse to leave their children behind, so they remain in the group. At other times, even though one parent leaves the cult, the other may stay. In most of those cases, the children remain, too.

Rita Tupper joined Jim Jones' organization, the Peoples Temple in California in 1969. Her eleven-year-old boy, Tim, became good friends with Stephan, Jim Jones' son. Tim's dad divorced his mom soon after she joined the cult. She kept three daughters and the outgoing Tim with her while her ex-husband kept custody of their other two sons. A few months later Tim moved into the Jones household. Jim Jones taught that all children of cult members were Peoples Temple property, and he told the boy not to have anything to do with his mother and sisters. Six years later he was officially adopted by Jones and his wife.

At seventeen, Tim moved to Jonestown, the Temple's settlement in the remote jungles of Guyana. There he became head of security. Part of his job was to bring women members to his adopted father in the middle of the night so Jones could have sex with them. One of the women Tim was ordered to secretly usher into Jones' bedroom was his own girlfriend. He didn't protest, because he'd been taught since he was a child to obey Jones without question.

Tim was in Georgetown, Guyana's capital on November 18, 1978, when Jones gave the order, "We're going to see Mrs. Frazier," which meant that it was time for members to swallow grape drink mixed with cyanide. This time he didn't obey. Six days later, Tim was flown by the government to identify the decomposing bodies of believers scattered everywhere—913 of them. Nearly everyone he knew had perished in the tragedy.

4

Selling Salvation

Even when we are aware of why some people are more vulnerable to cults than others, most of us still have a difficult time imagining why anybody in their right mind would volunteer for a life of slavery. Why give up friends, family, and freedom in order to blindly follow a leader who asks you to lie, steal, and possibly kill? Because cults are often secretive about their recruiting methods, many myths surround them. Read over the following statements, and then mark your answers on another sheet of paper to see how much you know about cult recruitment.

_____ 1. Cults use physical force to recruit members.
_____ 2. Cult recruiters use brainwashing to get people to join.
_____ 3. People who join cults are asking for what they get.
_____ 4. Most people aren't easily fooled by a damaging cult, so they don't need to worry about being recruited into such a group.

What did you think? Compare your answers with the ones below.

1. **Cults use physical force to recruit members—Myth.** People join cults of their own free will. They are not kidnapped or beaten into dedicating their lives to a group. Cult members know that they can attract more recruits with friendliness than with threats. They also understand that giving people the illusion of choice at the beginning guarantees that those who do remain will be loyal. Only after people have actually become part of the cult are harsh methods of control sometimes used to keep them from asking questions or quitting.

2. **Cult recruiters use brainwashing to get people to join—Myth.** Cult recruiters create confusion and illusion. They trick potential converts into trusting them, hiding the true purpose of the group. Many of the tactics they use are the same ones practiced by salespeople and advertisers. These methods are better called *unfair persuasion* rather than *brainwashing,* which is a term for the forced indoctrination invented by the Chinese communists. Brainwashing involves physical torture to wipe prisoners' mental slates clean and then filling their minds with new beliefs. Victims of brainwashing are helpless to fight what is happening. Even though they are being unfairly influenced, targets of cult recruiting can choose not to join.

3. **People who join cults are asking for what they get—Myth.** Since cult recruiters are rarely honest about the goals and workings of their groups, new members don't *know* what they're getting into. Saying that cult members have asked for it is like saying battered women want to be beaten—a way of blaming the victim and ignoring the problem. Instead of feeling sympathy for victims of cults, people tend to make fun of them, often believing that they are weak, stupid, or emotionally sick. As we saw in Chapter 3, the opposite

is true. Cult leaders look for recruits who will contribute to the group.

4. **Most people aren't easily fooled by a damaging cult, so they don't need to worry about being recruited into such a group—Myth.** Any human being can be tricked by cult recruiters. We all have a need to feel good about ourselves. We need affection and to feel like we belong. Cult recruiters know how to meet those needs for us. They also know that in certain situations, all people automatically react in very predictable ways. Psychologists call these reactions *automatic behavior patterns*. Cults are expert at manipulating situations so people will join without stopping to think of the consequences. In addition to distorting reality by lying, creating illusions, and playing on human nature, recruiters also create altered states of consciousness and use group pressure to convince their listeners.

Divine Deception

Successful cult recruiters don't say, "Hi there, I belong to a cult, and I'd like you to give us the best years of your life. In return you'll be emotionally abused and possibly malnourished." If the cult recruiters told the truth, they'd never get new members for the group.

Think about it. If you *really* wanted to sell someone a car with no brakes, would you tell them the brakes didn't work? Would you take them for a test drive? If you were a good con artist, you'd first try to gain their *confidence* or trust in you. (That's where the *con* in *con artist* comes from.) Next you'd point out all the good features on the car. You might even start the engine, but if your potential customer mentioned brakes or driving around the block, you'd quickly switch the subject.

Of course, *you'd* never try to sell someone a dangerous vehicle. Most cult members weren't dishonest people either, not before they became enmeshed in a damaging group and their values changed. Cults place high emphasis on increasing membership, rewarding successful recruiters. Failure to win new members results in shame and punishment as severe as going without food or beatings. Recruiting new cult members is a great deal like selling broken down cars on commission.

It is no wonder cult recruiters conceal the truth and tell outright lies in order to trap the unsuspecting. Because they are taught that lying to help the cult and its leader isn't wrong, they will use every unethical trick in the book to convince people to join. They practice what members of the Unification Church call *divine deception.*

Some cult recruiters spend their days on the streets, pretending to collect money for causes such as helping the homeless, feeding the hungry, or fighting drugs. They infiltrate organizations like Bible-study fellowships and college campus groups that work to improve the world in order to get to know people and invite them to attend a cult event. They may even sneak into your home. Several damaging cults have members working as house cleaners or babysitters in order to establish close contact with new targets for recruitment.

Other places you might encounter cult recruiters are:

- at school;
- at parties, dances, restaurants, sports events and after-school hang-outs;
- in classes and seminars, especially those that talk about self-improvement or ways to manage stress;
- in hospitals.

Cult members usually approach targets and start a conversation. This leads to "friendship." Next comes an invitation to attend a discussion group, party, class, or weekend retreat sponsored by the cult. There the newcomer is surrounded with yet more "friends" and asked to attend more activities. Only later, will the true nature of the group slowly be revealed over weeks or months.

Occasionally damaging cults resort to very complex deceptions. The Brooklyn Greens are a case in point. Few could argue with the flyers that appeared in the upscale neighborhoods of Park Slope and Brooklyn Heights during the spring of 1988. "We believe in social responsibility, ecological wisdom, care for others and respect for life," they read. The flyers were signed by the Brooklyn Greens, a self-proclaimed neighborhood activist group that wanted to stop the construction of a large trash incinerator at the Brooklyn Navy Yard.

Within months, the group attracted a number of members who met once a week, held rallies, and helped circulate petitions. They opened a store-front office, which drew even more people to the fight against pollution. Most assumed that the Brooklyn Greens were associated with the Green Party in Western Europe, a well-established group working for environmental and anti-nuclear causes.

Even if the bright, well-educated volunteers had questions, there was no time to ask them. Nicole and Jean-Marc Grambert, the leaders, monopolized their time. Nicole talked to men who wandered into the office while Jean-Marc gave the women his soulful gaze. There were phones to answer, meetings to attend, and banners to make, not to mention the long rambling lectures Jean-Marc gave on history and society. Only after a month did the truth begin to leak out—money for the project came from something called the Movement. Exhausted from all their work and excited by their progress toward blocking the incinerator, most volunteers didn't pay attention to that news. They should have.

When the Gramberts held a workshop on nonviolence for volunteers led by a man called the Orientor, those who attended were told to remove their watches. They were then bombarded with questions. "What is suffering?" and "What is happiness?" Next came lengthy readings from philosophers. Afterward they were ordered to write revealing essays about their own experiences with violence, which they shared with others. Finally they were instructed to play a series of physical and role-playing games that encouraged them to trust and reveal their deepest fears.

By the end of the workshop, some were so physically and emotionally exhausted that they sobbed and screamed. As they put on their coats to go home, they were told that the only solution to their personal despair was something called the Movement. The literature they were handed explained that the Brooklyn Greens were part of the Movement, which was run by a man named Silo who taught a combination of meditation and revolution. The group had no connection with the Green Party of Europe as many had assumed. Instead the name had deliberately been stolen to gain their confidence.

What they *weren't* told that night was that the Movement, an international cult begun in 1969 in Chile, had attracted an estimated 12,000 members in Europe, North and South America, and Asia by 1988. Neither did they know that twice a year, they would need to give at least $140 to support the group or that, in order to get ahead in the organization, they had to focus all their time and attention on recruiting new members. They had no idea that Silo's stated goal was to take over the environmental movement and, using that base, break down all existing belief systems and take over the world.

Had they known the truth when they first walked into the Brooklyn Green's office, chances are, many members would have run right out the door. Silo's goals were opposed to their own values. As it happened, by the time the hidden agenda leaked out in bits and pieces, they had already made a commitment of time and energy, protesting the incinerator. Worn out and confused by the end of the nonviolence workshop, they were ready to ignore their better judgment and promise to be part of the Movement. After the next step—donating money and working directly for the Movement—most would become so deeply involved that Silo's goals would become their own.

Few of us would suspect that an ecology group was a front for cult recruitment, yet it was. The Movement isn't the only cult that disguises itself in this way. Scientologists routinely send out flyers to doctors and dentists, advertising free, three-hour management training seminars held by a company called Sterling Management, a cult-owned company. Of course, the word *Scientology* is never mentioned on the brochure.

Something for Nothing

When he first signed up for them, the Sterling Management workshops sounded like a good deal to Dr. Robert Geary, an unsuspecting dentist in Ohio. After the first free workshop, Geary was asked to take a personality test, then told he could improve his practice and make more money if he attended a week-long class in California. He wrote the company a check for more than $10,000. Next he was pressured to sign up for Scientology classes in San Francisco. Here Geary was ordered to separate from his wife and was subjected to hours of psychological exercises like "bull-bating" where he had to sit and stare for hours at another person without moving or talking. "Those kinds of exercises were making me emotionless," he says today, "It was like I didn't have a mind of my own."

The Scientologists kept demanding more money and even forged the dentist's signature on a $20,000 check. Then they moved into his Ohio house so they could work on him around the clock. Cult members held his wife captive in a cabin on the West Coast for two weeks, telling her she was being held hostage to correct behavior that could harm the organization. Within five months of the first free seminar, the dentist had given away $200,000, and his wife was so upset, she needed psychiatric help. Dr. and Mrs. Geary survived their ordeal, and despite an offer from Sterling Management to pay them $44,000 for their silence, the couple continues to talk. Says Geary, "I hope that we can prevent other people from making the same mistake we did."

The mistake the Gearys made and that thousands of other cult victims make each year is assuming that they are being offered something for nothing. Cult members give things to those they are trying to con. The gift might be a no-cost seminar or lecture like the one promised by Sterling Management, or it may be a free book, trip, retreat, or meal. These offers have strings attached. Cult recruiters know that when they present us with a "gift," we'll feel we owe them something. It doesn't matter that we didn't ask for the present or that we don't really want it, we still feel obligated to give something back to our benefactor. This is an automatic human behavior pattern that psychologists call *reciprocation*.

The rule of reciprocation is a facet of our daily lives. How would you feel if a friend handed you a Christmas present, and you hadn't thought to buy him or her one? If your friend told you not to worry, that your friendship was the best gift, would you relax and enjoy the present? Or would you feel guilty and want to rush out to buy a more expensive gift to make up for your forgetfulness?

Most of us don't feel right taking something for nothing because we've been taught that to do so isn't polite. In order to feel good about ourselves, we return favors without hesitation. If we don't, we'll feel obligated to the other person. This automatic response is even stronger when we accept a gift in front of other people.

Cult members use reciprocation as bait. If a recruiter takes us to a free lecture, we may feel obligated, out of politeness, to stay up all night for the discussion that follows even though we really want to be home in bed. The payment that a good cult recruiter will try to collect at this point usually isn't a promise to join the cult. It's much too early for that. More likely we'll be asked to attend another, more intense, presentation like the "non-violence" workshop held for the Movement recruitees. The price may be attending a weekend retreat away from friends and family where we can be more easily influenced. On the surface, this invitation appears to be yet another gift, making us feel even more obligated. In fact, when cult recruiters invite us to activities, they are doing us *no* favor at all.

Love at First Sight

Love makes the world go around and cult recruiters know it. They understand that not only do most humans want love—we *need* it because love is an essential ingredient for emotional health. Without love, infants who are physically heathy can die from what doctors call *failure to thrive syndrome.* Low self-esteem, depression, and other emotional problems have all been tied by mental health experts to lack of love. We like to be around people who show us affection and respect, and we avoid those who show the opposite. Even when we have enough love in our lives to survive, most of us seem to want just a bit more. Cult members are experts at creating the illusion of love. The word they use for this strategy is *love bombing.*

When Jamal first met George at the mall, he was put off by the other teenager's instant friendliness. After all, how often does a stranger walk up, compliment you on your sweatshirt, strike up a conversation, and then try to get you to agree to come to a meeting all in ten minutes? In the four days between their first encounter and the meeting, George called three times. He was easy to talk with and seemed genuinely interested in Jamal's thoughts and his life. No one else had ever seemed so eager before to listen to his hopes and dreams for the future. His doubts began to lessen, and soon he felt as though the friendship had been destined.

The night George drove him to the meeting, Jamal felt more optimistic than he had in a long time. "I know you're going to like the meeting," George said. "Our group is a lot like peer counseling at the high school. It's rough to survive these days, man." And then he confided, "You're going to learn some things that will transform your life."

The people at the self-help circle clustered around Jamal as soon as he entered the room, smiling, meeting his eyes, shaking his hand, and patting him in the back. Each one had a compliment. When the lecture for the evening turned out to be on ending gang violence, once more it seemed to him as if fate were at work, so it didn't really matter that he didn't understand many of the terms the speaker used. What counted was the good feeing in the room. Besides, George reassured him that if he kept coming back, everything would fall into place. Jamal felt honored to be chosen to attend a training session that the group was holding in the mountains over spring break. The thought that George might be trying to get him involved in a cult, or that his new friends had ulterior motives never entered Jamal's mind.

Flattery like that Jamal experienced is difficult for anyone to resist. As a rule of thumb, if you think people seem too good to be true, chances are, you're right— they're probably putting on an act. Trust and emotional intimacy don't happen instantly, not in the real world. Love-bombing techniques—including eye contact, touching, hugging, giving unconditional approval, and listening to every word we speak—get us feeling so good about ourselves and the people love bombing us, that we actually get an emotional high from this make-believe caring which weakens our defenses and makes us easy prey.

Unfriendly Persuasion

If we were gathering information, weighing all the options, and thinking about consequences, few of us would join a group that asked for all our time and money while giving very little in return. Sure, we might feel obligated to people who treat us well—but not *that* obligated. And we'd all feel a little dizzy with an overdose of flattery and attention—but not *that* dizzy. Most of us, when we put our minds to it, can make reasonably sound decisions for ourselves, even when others try to influence us.

Damaging cults don't want us to think. If we're not thinking, we won't have second thoughts about joining. Our feelings are more easily manipulated than our thoughts. Cult recruiters bring out heavy ammunition designed to drive us out of our rational minds, make us more emotional, and drive us into their groups before we know what's happened.

Although manipulation tactics vary, usually the most intense recruiting takes place during all-night meetings or weekend retreats. Unethical persuasion is most effective when victims are tired and away from familiar surroundings, including contact with friends and family members. Under these conditions, damaging cults can create any illusion they choose without outside interference. While not all workshops and retreats sponsored by these cults are the same, all of them are planned to take advantage of people. Cult recruiters use the following tools to exert unfair influence on the people who attend.

Alertness Stopping

Lack of sleep and a diet high in sugar unbalance our bodies and our minds. Think about the last time you stayed up all night studying for a test, trying to keep yourself awake by drinking one caffeine- and sugar-filled soft drink after another. Chances are, you weren't in top form the next day. You may have felt like you were moving in a fog.

Cult retreats and workshops are usually crammed with planned activities designed to keep people awake for long periods of time. Sessions like the one held by the Movement run far into the night so that attendees are too busy fighting off sleep to be fully aware of what is happening around them. Feeding participants high-sugar foods ensures that they'll get a sugar "rush," a short-term burst of energy to the brain that is followed by a dramatic drop in blood-sugar, or glucose. Because glucose fuels the brain cells, a drop in glucose clouds thinking and makes people even more tired and less able to focus.

Physical discomfort also lowers alertness. Often cult recruiters ask people at meetings or workshops to sit in one position for hours without giving them a break to stretch their muscles. Others allow participants no time to use the restroom. The stronger our physical discomfort grows, the more we pay attention to the painful sensations inside our bodies, ignoring the outside clues that let us know we are in a risky situation.

Programmed Confusion

Unfamiliar surroundings cause us to become disoriented and make us dependent on others who appear to know where they're going and what will happen next. Under these circumstances, most of us follow the leader without much question. Handily, cults often provide a buddy or big "sister" or "brother" to accompany a potential member through the next few hours or days. The more confused and disoriented that person becomes, the more he or she must depend on the buddy in order to survive the weekend.

Damaging cults purposely keep people off balance by making them rush from one activity to another with no clue of what is to come. This feeling of being out of control is made worse when we lose track of time. For this reason cult recruiters usually don't have clocks at meetings and retreats. If you show up wearing a watch, you'll probably be asked to remove it.

Reality and illusion are further merged by providing participants with too much information for their brains to process at one time. Imagine trying to hold a conversation on the phone with the TV blaring and the radio on high volume in the next room. If you think that would be difficult, imagine how you'd feel if the cat and dog started fighting, the door bell rang and the kitchen sink overflowed all at the same time, too. More than likely, you'd try to focus on one thing at a time, but when everything demanded your immediate attention, your brain would spin with an overdose of confusion. "I can't think straight!" you'd complain. And you'd be right—you *couldn't* think straight because you were a victim of what psychologists call *sensory overload.*

The "facts" given to overload participants' minds are carefully controlled. Not all of them are true, but one thing is certain—there are plenty of them and they are complicated. Lectures are crammed with mind-numbing statistics, lists, and drawings. Listeners will be told they must remember it all, down to the last detail, even if they are confused. When they voice their confusion, they are either told everything will become clear to them later or they will be treated as though they are stupid. Most people suffer through the sensory overload in silence because they don't want to appear ignorant in front of their new friends.

Thought Stopping

Cult recruiters don't just want our brains to spin, they want them to go on strike completely. This occurs when we enter an *altered state of consciousness.* During an altered state of consciousness, we remain somewhat aware of events around us, but we aren't thinking about them because our minds are off somewhere else. When this happens we're extremely vulnerable to the suggestions other people make.

Altered states of consciousness commonly happen when people take drugs or drink alcohol, but cults have other methods that work just as well. Some of these are: meditation and breathing exercises, chanting and singing, and special lighting or sound effects. Any rhythmic sound or action tends to alter consciousness. Because the mechanical act of writing is a rhythmic activity that produces a similar effect, participants may be asked to copy long passages of written material. Speakers at retreats and meetings may deliberately talk in monotonous tones, almost like the ones hypnotists use. Others play music with a strong beat in the background. A leader may get people singing and then have them clap their hands or stomp their feet in time to the music.

Altering consciousness isn't always a bad thing. When you've been upset or frightened, has anyone ever told you to take deep breaths? Deep, rhythmic breathing has a calming effect on people—it alters their consciousness from a state of anxiety to one of relative calm. Mood-alterers like deep breathing work because they cause the body to release neurotransmitters called *endorphins,* or natural opiates. Endorphins help calm us and relieve pain, just as opiates do. Some researchers even call the positive feelings we get from these neurotransmitters natural highs.

Altering consciousness becomes dangerous when people use it to influence us in unethical ways. When former cult members report that the meetings and retreats during which they decided to join the group were one of the most intense emotional highs that they've ever felt, they aren't exaggerating. Telling tired, hungry, and information-overloaded people to chant the same phrase for hours while sitting under pulsing stobe lights, makes them extremely susceptible to the cult message that follows.

Intense Emotional Stimulation

Messages preached by cult leaders appeal to the emotions rather than the intellect. Audiences are told they'll benefit from cooperating with the group to fight against a common enemy such as poverty, war, or parents who don't understand their teenagers. Emotionally charged words such as *freedom, injustice,* and *evil,* are used to paint a gloomy picture of the world and a blissful picture of how the world could be if a potential member joined. Bible passages may be quoted to stir further emotion.

Most of the emotional appeals that damaging cults make would have seemed childish to us if we heard them during the first encounter with the recruiter. At meetings and retreats, however, leaders often try to trick us into seeing things as being black or white. The group of people we're with at this retreat is good, we're told. Our old friends are bad. The workshop speakers are telling the truth. Up until now, we've been told nothing but lies.

Cult leaders manipulate their potential victims into thinking like children by making them behave like children. This is called *regression.* Weekend activities at cult recruiting camp that push people to think like children include children's games, water fights, sports, coloring, and singing children's songs.

Little children are easily led because they haven't yet gained the ability to be critical thinkers who can detect flawed logic. They don't have enough experience to make sensible predictions about the possible consequences of their choices. They can also be more easily confused and made unsure of themselves than adults.

Group Pressure to Conform

Resisting peer pressure from friends who say smoking won't hurt you and that everybody drinks, isn't easy. Teenagers and many adults have difficulty saying no to people they want to impress. Cult recruiters are experts at making a good impression, using group pressure tactics to get their way.

The first step of peer pressure involves getting us to identify with the group. Individual cult members are taught to convince newcomers that they have stumbled onto the best friends that they'll ever have by probing for interests, likes, and dislikes. If you can't stand canned peas, your retreat buddy will hate them every bit as much as you do. If you like science fiction movies, your buddy will too. After a while you might think, "Hey, these are people just like me!"

Not quite. By this time you will have heard a number of words you never heard before. Cult members use unfamiliar terms called *jargon* to create the impression that newcomers are part of a special group that has secret, exclusive knowledge. Most people want to be in on the secret so they can feel special, too. When we find people who are like us in every way but one—they are part of the in club and we aren't—we want to become insiders. It's another automatic behavior pattern.

Audiences at cult meetings and retreats are often planted with *ringers,* members who pretend to be newcomers. These ringers talk about all the good things the organization has done for them and agree with points the lecturer makes. "Our society is sick," the speaker might proclaim. "Yes," a ringer will shout and then go on to provide examples that are stunningly similar to things you've experienced. Often a ringer is the first one in the audience to make a public commitment to the group.

If members of the audience still have doubts, the skilled acting of ringers can erase them with *social proof,* yet another automatic behavior pattern. We're more likely to believe a certain way when we know other people believe that way as well. Their belief is proof or evidence that what we think is right. The more similar we believe others to be to us, the stronger the social proof they provide us and the more it affects us in our decision making.

Provoking a Crisis

Positive emotions aren't the only ones stirred by cult recruiters. Once people are experiencing an emotional high, events may quickly turn ugly. Attendees may be led to fear something terrible will happen to them if they don't believe the cult message and act on it right away. Sometimes these threats are stated outright. A cult member may tell you the end of the world is just around the corner or that you could be dying right now from a horrible illness and not know it. Other times, doom may only be hinted at.

Newcomers are made to feel guilty for their lives so far and urged to make confessions in front of the group about all of the things they've done wrong in the past. Consider how nervous you feel when you're called to present a report in front of one of your classes at school. The anxiety you'd feel if you had to stand up in front of new friends and confess to every bad thought you'd had in the last month, say, would be about a hundred times stronger. When people admit in public that they are shameful, pitiful human beings, often their self-esteem erodes to the point where they will do anything to gain relief—even join a cult. They probably won't realize that actions of the group are what caused them to feel so hopeless in the first place.

At this stage in the cult recruiting game, group leaders often make an example of one or two people in the crowd by making fun of them or verbally abusing them to the point of tears. Sometimes the scapegoat is chosen because he or she has asked too many questions or doesn't quite fit in. Others are selected because of doubts they expressed to their buddy, someone they were encouraged to trust completely. When this happens, it appears almost as though the leader can read people's minds. Even to *think* rebellious thoughts is dangerous.

When Bonita was invited to an intensive Bible-study camp by the woman she'd come to regard as her substitute mother, she was excited because it would give her a chance to make some friends who shared her new beliefs. Once she was there, though, some doubts began to surface. When she disagreed with some of the speaker's points during a lecture, she stood up and politely said so. She wasn't prepared for his reaction. "You're nothing but a worm. You're lower than a worm," the man shouted.

"I'm not," she protested, angry because he sounded like

her mom when she was drunk. "I'm not saying that I'm better than everybody here, but I'm not all bad either. I just can't believe everything you're saying."

"You're worse than hopeless, and you were doomed to hell before you were even born," the man continued. As Bonita looked around the room, she saw others nodding in agreement. She wanted to stand and fight, but she was outnumbered. Besides, she'd come to the retreat on a bus provided by the group and had yet to see a phone to call her dad. Few cars passed by on the road that lay a mile from the buildings. She could try to walk home, but she wasn't sure her hosts would let her leave. Bonita wished she'd never come, but it was too late now. Hands shaking, she slunk down on the hard, metal chair. Although Bonita tried to silently resist group pressure, she couldn't. Her example was also a powerful persuader to other people to conform.

The isolation at many cult recruiting events is a potent manipulation tool. From hints to demands, newcomers are encouraged to cut their ties with the past, including friends and close family. Those who attend these events are often made to burn their bridges symbolically. The activity might consist of writing a letter to a boyfriend or girlfriend, breaking off the relationship. People are sometimes asked to select something important to them, like a picture of a family member, and destroy it in front of the group as a way to show they are ready for a new life. For someone looking for the strength to gain independence from parents, this can seem empowering, but once ties are cut, even symbolically, there is nowhere to go for help and support except to the group.

Getting a Commitment

Near the point of breakdown from riding the roller coaster of cult-manipulated emotions, most people are ready to jump at the remedy recruiters offer—making a decision to remain with the group. Usually recruiters don't press for complete commitment. Instead they work up to that point one small step at a time, getting recruits to join by default. They may never say, "Yes, I'll join," but they never say *no* either.

"Do you want to be happy?" the recruiter asks.

Of course you can't disagree. Everybody does. "Yes," you say. (You've been fooled into making a commitment to something you have no need to commit to.)

"You love God, don't you?"

The recruiter means the cult's definition of God, but how are you ever going to be able to make the blanket statement that you *don't* love God at a spiritual retreat? "I guess so," you reply, making the second commitment.

"You guess so?"

"I know so, but . . ." (You've been hooked again.)

"You want to know more about God, don't you?"

"Yes, but . . . ."

"You love and want to know more about God because you understand that it is the path to true happiness." As the recruiter speaks, you nod in agreement. "Then what could be the harm in staying another week with us and learning more?"

"But I have to go to school," you protest weakly. "And my parents will worry."

"Your parents want you to know about God, don't they?" Maybe giving in is the only way to get the recruiter to ever stop bugging you. "We only invite special people for the advanced classes."

"Later in the summer, okay?"

"The workshops starting tomorrow are the only ones this year," the recruiter lies. You want to go home, but you feel torn by this one-time offer. "Of course, if you don't care about God. . . ." The recruiter's voice trails off.

"I'll stay."

Once you've said those two little words, the chances are high that you won't change your mind and back out. Chances are high, as well, that you'll agree to the next commitment the recruiter asks you to make whether it's to attend a two-month camp or to move into a house with other cult members.

When human beings make a commitment, even a small one like agreeing that they want to be happy, it colors the way they see themselves. Once we've taken a stand in front of other people by raising a hand, getting to our feet, or promising to do something, our self-image suffers if we back out. This tendency is the result of another automatic human behavior pattern called *consistency*. According to the rule of consistency, once we've made even a small pledge of time or money or have vowed to do something for the group, the recruiter's job is over. We've been sold.

After we've kept the promise, no one needs to pressure us into going further. We do that all by ourselves because we now have a *vested interest* in the group. Our loyalty to it will increase right along with our vested interest. The people who volunteered for the Brooklyn Greens felt it would be foolish to back out, even when they learned that they'd been lied to, because they'd already spent a great deal of time working for the group. To quit then would mean, not only that they had wasted their time, but that they had been foolish. Once Dr. Geary had paid for the second Sterling Management seminar, if he quit he would have had been admitting that he'd thrown his money away. He would have seen himself as a poor decision maker and a wasteful person. Continuing to sign up for seminars to try to actually receive something for the money he was spending seemed to make more sense at that point. With every check he wrote, he strengthened his reasons for staying.

5

Life Inside a
Damaging Cult

The details about why more than fifty men, women, and children who had been members of the Order of the Solar Temple in Switzerland and Canada would take their own lives remain a mystery. That riddle is hauntingly similar to the questions still being asked months after the tragedy in Waco.

Many Americans still remain puzzled about the raid, 51-day siege, and suicide/murders at David Koresh's Branch Davidian compound in Texas. Some cult and law enforcement experts have expressed doubts about the wisdom of the first raid by Alcohol, Tobacco, and Firearms experts and the full-scale assault a month and a half later. At the time, cult members were assumed to be held against their wills—once a show of force gave them a chance to leave, they would peaceably march from the compound to surrender. Most people didn't think that the Branch

Davidians were so loyal to Koresh that they would obey *any* order he gave them, even a demand to kill others and take their own lives.

Neither could people understand why the Branch Davidians had given up all financial independence by turning paychecks, Social Security checks, and food stamps over to Koresh. In return they received the "honor" of giving their wives to the leader. Koresh had even hinted that the lives of their children might be the next offering he demanded. One Australian man who left the cult reported that David Koresh had asked him how far he was prepared to go in his commitment. When the man looked bewildered, Koresh had said, "Which of your children are you prepared to sacrifice?"

Cult members were fed only small amounts, worked until they were exhausted, and then endured hours of lectures by their leader. Their self-styled savior lived by a different set of rules. Koresh ate steaks, drank beer, watched MTV, and took as many wives as he pleased while forbidding husbands and wives among his followers to sleep together. His reason for this, he told them, was that all the women in the world belonged to him alone. Some of his wives were rumored to be only eleven or twelve years old.

David Koresh taught that he was the new messiah, one who, unlike the old one, lived *with* sin. A former cult member told reporters that Koresh claimed God had to send down a sinful Jesus so that on Judgment Day, he'd have enough experience with wrongdoing to know how to evaluate them properly.

Even after the fiery inferno destroyed Koresh and his followers, several cult members who had been away from the compound gave statements to reporters, praising Koresh and his actions. Some even expressed guilt that they had missed out on being destroyed. Now they would have to wait to die a natural death to make their way to heaven.

The fact that so many people went along with Koresh seems bizarre because behavior like this appears to go against everything we've learned since birth about how human beings usually act. Even when we understand how people get tricked into joining a cult, it may be difficult to fully understand why they don't escape when they are being treated brutally. We wonder why they don't over-throw their leader if he is obviously insane. If the studies of cult researchers are true, once these cult members were bright, idealistic people, looking for meaning in their lives and trying to make the world a better place. How could their values change so drastically that they could kill other people and themselves without a second thought?

In the years that have passed since the mass suicides of more than 900 followers of the charismatic leader Jim Jones, people still ask many of the same questions they do about the Branch Davidians. Members of the Peoples Temple had hints that tragedy was about to happen. In San Francisco in 1973, even before he moved the group to the remote jungles of Guyana, Jim Jones brought up the idea of mass suicide at an emergency meeting of the Temple's Emer-gency Planning Commission. He suggested that everyone take poison then, promising that followers would be united on another planet. "This might be the time for all of us to make our translation together," he told them. They could have left the cult then, but they didn't. Instead, they chose to stay and support him.

Three years later, when the Peoples Temple was still based in Northern California, Jones ordered members of the Planning Commission to drink a glass of wine. They were shocked because Temple rules forbade alcohol, but they did as their leader told them to do. As soon as they'd finished, Jones announced that the wine was poisoned and they would die in an hour. When the hour passed, and no one had died, and Jones explained there was no poison in the wine, followers assumed he had been testing the strength of their loyalty to him and to the group. They could have walked away then, too, but their loyalty increased.

Despite the fact that Jones punished people harshly, they followed him to the jungle without question. They continued to believe he was God as he claimed, and they obeyed his every whim, even though strong evidence existed that he was addicted to several drugs, including amphetamines and Percodan, a narcotic painkiller.

In the meantime, stories about abuses at Jonestown began filtering back to the United States. A group calling itself Concerned Relatives, feared for the safety of their family members who had become Jones' followers. Some of them had defected from the cult earlier and wanted to get their children back. They claimed that cult members were being held against their will. To help them free their relatives, they had enlisted the support of Congressman Leo Ryan, who flew to Guyana to investigate along with two staffers and a four-person NBC news crew.

When the group of investigators arrived at Jonestown, most cult members claimed to be happy—they just wanted to be left alone. Congressman Ryan's group was fed dinner and treated to a concert by the Jonestown Band. The next day, when they tried to leave, they were gunned down at the airstrip. Ryan and three members of the news crew were killed along with one woman, a cult member trying to leave Jonestown. Ten people were wounded.

After the shooting and shortly before the mass suicide in Jonestown began, Jim Jones radioed his followers in Georgetown, miles away, asking if they had any poison. When they told him no, he suggested they should take their lives. Sharon Amos, a young mother who ran the public relations office in Georgetown, slit her children's throats and then used a knife on herself.

Even though group pressure might be too hard for some to resist, when Peoples Temple members began drinking the poison-laced grape drink, why did no one put a stop to the madness? And why would someone like Sharon Amos, many miles away from Jim Jones and the compound, brutally kill her children and herself?

Waco and Jonestown are extreme examples of how life in a cult changes people. Most damaging cults do not demand their members perform acts of violence on themselves or others. They do expect members to lie when they recruit new members and to use any means possible to obtain money for the organization. No matter what order a leader gives, members are expected to follow it, cutting themselves off from their past beliefs about right and wrong to follow a new one—the end justifies the means.

- In 1993, Fuqra, a small cult in Colorado Springs, was charged with submitting fraudulent workmen's compensation claims. After members obtained money by lying to the government, they laundered the money and then invested it in property the group bought for a headquarters.
- In Tucson in 1991, a yoga instructor and self-styled guru named Waress Muskkir was convicted of arson, theft by extortion, fraud and criminal damage. He had plotted to get money from his followers by cheating insurance companies and had threatened to kill members if they didn't come up with money.

  A former member, a news anchor at a local TV station, who testified against him, said that she'd written bad checks. She'd also lied to her insurance company and police about $60,000 worth of jewelry she claimed had been stolen from her in order to collect insurance money. She'd gone from door to door raising money she said was for Toys for Tots; in reality she gave the money to her guru. A printer testified that he had lied about a burglary at his business and filed a false insurance claim. He also tried to extort over $100,000 from a lawyer. Both said they believed Muskkir had supernatural powers and could read their minds.
- In late 1991, two women members of a group called the Jesus Cathedral were arrested for child abuse. Church services, held in a rented room at an airport, included

whipping four-year-old children with telephone cords. Children interviewed by police officers said they were told these beatings were the will of God. When the kids acted up, their parents would write "Demon be out of me!" and beat their sons and daughters until they repeated the phrase.

When we hear about the behavior of cult members such as these, most of us are absolutely certain that *we* would have rebelled. Promising to attend the next meeting or even to work with them is much different than making such a strong commitment to the group and its beliefs that we do things we never would have considered before joining. Under normal circumstances, most of us *would* rebel, but cult life presents us with circumstances far from normal.

Frank reluctantly allowed Judy to drag him along to one of the self-improvement classes and was bored the entire evening—all the people did there was listen to the leader and take notes as though everything the woman said was important. He thought her ideas about preparing for the end of the world were pretty stupid. On the way home, he told Judy, even though he loved her, he'd never go again.

That summer she followed her fellow believers to what was to be a month-long survival camp at the group's headquarters in a neighboring state. Although she promised to write when she left, the entire month went by with no letters. After she hadn't returned in six weeks, Frank became worried. Maybe she was being held prisoner, he thought, so he decided to visit in order to see for himself.

Once he saw her, he became even more concerned. Judy had changed drastically. She seemed too serious, but there was something strange about her seriousness. Her face showed no expression, and her eyes were blank, as though someone had stolen her soul. The few times he managed to speak to her in private, she refused his suggestion that she should come home. When he was asked to participate in the survival exercises and then to remain for the rest of the summer, he agreed in order to have a chance to talk some sense into her.

Over the next few weeks, Frank was allowed to spend very little time alone with Judy. Between attending lectures, working to help build more cabins on the grounds and participating in training exercises, he was so exhausted that the summer passed in a blur. Frank liked all the physical activity even if he didn't agree with the group's purposes. He was in better shape now than he could ever remember. A few of the people he lived with weren't so bad, and he had to admit the survival drills were exciting, especially target practices with real guns. He'd never fired a gun before, but he found he was an excellent shot. Frank hadn't had so much fun since he was a little kid playing army. At the end of July he wrote a letter to his parents saying he'd be home in the fall.

In the days and weeks that passed, he didn't actually forget his original mission to save Judy, but he was so busy that he thought about it less and less often. By October, he hadn't gone home yet. When he was asked by one of the group leaders to help install a security system that would wound and might even kill trespassers on the property, he didn't think twice. If trespassers invaded, they deserved to die.

Every aspect of day-to-day cult life is aimed at bringing about a 180 degree turn in member's values. As beliefs start to shift and the cult member gets caught up in a whirlwind of activity, not only do values and standards of behavior change, old ones are repressed or held down. Members grow so completely devoted to the cult leader that often they are willing to go to any length for admission to the inner circle, the small group of people closest to that person. Their behavior becomes robot-like as they carry out orders without thinking. They are no longer in control of their lives and their minds—the cult and its leader are. The reasons for this drastic change are many.

Group Pressure

Groups exert a great deal of power over their members. Whether we decide to join the Moonies or the basketball team at school, we have a vested interest in fitting in. If we didn't care what other members thought of us, we wouldn't be hanging around with them. It's only natural to want the other people in our group to continue to like us and accept us as one of them after they've allowed us to become insiders.

Even when the group is a small, informal one such as a clique of three or four friends, we still may feel like a minority of one if we refuse to do something the others want us to do. To go against the crowd, even a very small crowd, can be frightening, especially when we lack many strong ties to people outside the group. If our friends turned against us, we think we'll be outcasts. Sometimes, against our better judgment, we choose to do something we consider wrong rather than to live with the loneliness of rejection.

According to Michael D. Langone, director of research for the American Family Foundation, *all* groups, even the informal ones we encounter in everyday life, have the potential to harm people by influencing behavior. Groups sometimes use manipulative techniques that aren't in our best interests. The difference between damaging cults and most of the other groups we encounter in our lives is that damaging cults use group pressure to exploit and harm their members to a greater degree, one that isn't socially or ethically acceptable.

The first time Tina visited her biological father for the summer after her parents' divorce, she didn't know anybody but him in the town where he'd moved. Eventually she struck up a conversation with the older girls next door who asked her to go shopping with them. During the outing, she saw one shoplift a bottle of expensive perfume. Tina felt uncomfortable, but she didn't say anything. She'd never take anything and that was what counted, she told herself.

As the summer wore on, she spent more time with her neighbors. In a way she admired them. They were pretty, had lots of boyfriends, and seemed to know more about life than she did. She asked her dad to buy her some clothes like theirs and began copying the way they talked. She even started smoking pot occasionally. She was shocked when they all claimed to be Satan worshippers, but sharing that secret was exciting, too.

By the end of the summer, at the urging of her friends she began shoplifting. They all did it, so it couldn't be *that* bad, she rationalized. Besides, the first time, when she'd hesitated, they'd made fun of her. The more she shoplifted, the less afraid she became. In fact, she grew to like the excitement of stealing things. They assured her that she wouldn't be caught because they did protection rituals. Although Tina hadn't met the man who was her new friends' teacher, she did participate in casting some informal spells and curses.

A few weeks after Tina returned to her mother's house that fall, she could hardly believe she'd actually stolen things, smoked marijuana, put curses on people, and vowed to love the devil. Even though she hadn't felt any guilt during the summer, now she felt uneasy because the things she'd done were so unlike the kind of person she'd once thought herself to be. It was frightening to think how quickly she could change.

Nonetheless, she continued to write to her friends and made arrangements to visit her dad over Christmas vacation for the specific purpose of seeing them. Those friendships were something that belonged to her, something her mother couldn't interfere with. If she ever tried, she'd be getting more than she bargained for!

Forcing Commitment

Cults use many of the techniques that work for recruiting new members to force those who have joined into a deeper level of conversion and complete acceptance of the group's lifestyle. Psychologist Rosabeth Moss Kanter who has studied cults for over twenty years, has discovered six commitment tools that these groups use to turn ordinary people into obedient slaves.

Sacrifice

When people join cults they are usually asked to give up things that have given them pleasure in the past. Some groups warn their members not to drink or smoke. (This may not be such a bad thing!) Others tell new believers, even married couples, that sex is forbidden to them. Members may be asked to stop eating meat, going to movies, reading books, or watching TV. Studies show that the more people suffer to join a group, the more highly they value group membership.

Investment

Soon after members have been recruited, they may be told to give their life savings or belongings to the leader. As we saw earlier, the more a person invests in a group, the bigger the commitment he or she will make to it. When a destructive cult demands *all* of a new member's belongings, a much deeper commitment is forced. Without money of their own, people can't rent apartments or buy groceries. They become absolutely dependent on the group to take care of them and make choices about where they will live and what and when they will eat. Even small decisions like whether to spend ten dollars on a movie or use it to get a haircut are taken away from them.

Renunciation

Cult members are asked to turn their backs on the world outside. In some cults this renunciation is extreme. Newspapers and television are often forbidden to members. Members may be ordered, as had those of the Peoples Temple, to move miles away from the familiar. Cults with communal living facilities such as dormitories may require members to leave home and live there.

Damaging cults that allow members to live on their own still pressure them either to convert their families or cut off all contact with them. As new friendships are formed within the cult, cult members are ordered to give up their old friends. Sometimes they don't need to be told. Members frequently shun family and friends voluntarily because they share little in common with them. When people lose connection with the outside world, their identity as part of the group grows stronger. As that identity strengthens, they tend to see outsiders as enemies and to fear them.

Communion

Since groups recruit people with beliefs at least somewhat similar to their own, the people who join often share common backgrounds, and quickly form strong bonds with one another. As members become more and more indoctrinated into every aspect of a group's beliefs, their own beliefs become identical other members'. The feeling of connectedness grows and causes group pressure to have an even stronger effect. This feeling of communion intensifies to a point where cult members may even believe they can read each others' minds. Instead of seeing the truth, that they're being deliberately turned into carbon copies of one another, they often interpret this commonality as something mystical and otherworldly.

Mortification

The Synanon Game worked so well at changing the behavior of clients because it used *shame* to control victims' thoughts and feelings. Shame differs from the guilt many people feel when they make a mistake. When we feel guilt, we acknowledge that we've *done* wrong, knowing that we can either correct it or try to avoid it next time. When we feel shame, however, we believe we *are* mistakes, and that there's nothing we can do about it. People can cause us to feel shame by threatening to break their connection with us, implying that we're such terrible, unlovable people they want nothing to do with us. The more dependent for survival we are upon people who shame us, the more power they have to shape our behavior through humiliation. The threat of being cut off can be terrifying.

Members of a cult who must recite their sins in front of others and are repeatedly shamed form stronger ties to that cult. Believing themselves to be worthless, they soon suffer from what domestic violence counselors call *learned helplessness*. Because they're convinced that they can't function without the cult, they resolve to be whatever it defines as better people. Convinced that they are awful people who don't deserve love, they remain with the cult because they fear that no other group, not even their families, will ever want them. When people are humiliated in public and then forgiven, they feel so grateful, they may forget to be angry at the cult for humiliating them in the first place.

Transcendence

Ritual, which is used by most religions as a part of worship, is used by damaging cults as a means to further bind members to the group. Taking part in these rituals makes members feel special. They are among the chosen. Rituals also help to reinforce the idea that those who participate in them are an essential part of the community of believers. The tools to alter consciousness discussed in Chapter 4 are routine in many of these ceremonies or services.

Fasting, singing, chanting, drumming, and rhythmic breathing do more than halt thought. The mind-altering techniques discussed in Chapter 4 all can produce states of consciousness during which people may see visions or hear voices. As discussed earlier, there is nothing wrong with an altered state of consciousness in and of itself. In fact, most established religions and traditional belief systems in all cultures use some of these techniques as a regular part of worship and prayer. They teach that visions, voices, and dreams are God's way of speaking to believers. Sometimes people call these visions, voices, and dreams *mystical experiences.* They are more powerful than the usual events in our everyday lives and seem beyond scientific explanation.

Some psychologists and psychiatrists call these mystical experiences *hallucinations.* Their explanations for what causes some people to see and hear things that others don't range from chemical imbalances in the brain to insanity. If the latter were really true in all cases, more than half of the people in this country could be considered crazy by these disbelieving mental health professionals because most people in our culture think that at least some mystical experiences are communications from God. Many Americans say they have experienced them.

According to a 1987 Gallup Poll, nine out of ten people in this country believe in God. Forty percent of them say that God has spoken directly to them through some means. The same number say they know someone to whom God has spoken. A survey also conducted in 1987 by *Better Homes and Gardens* magazine found that eighty-six percent of the people questioned believed in miracles and seventy-three percent said they believed in direct communication from God to individuals.

Damaging religious cults take a different approach to mystical experiences than do traditional and established religions. These cults deprive members of sleep and food and deliberately use consciousness-altering techniques to *force* mystical experiences upon members. Cult members are then told that their visions come from the leader, rather than from God. These mystical experiences are always interpreted in ways that allow cult leaders to take more control over followers' lives and minds.

Destructive Cults and Mind Control

In addition to group pressure and forcing commitments from members who are not ready to make them, cults use a technique called *mind control* or *thought reform* to manipulate. In their first weeks of cult life, followers still keep many of their old beliefs as well as the illusion that they are making choices without unfair persuasion. At this stage, many have not actually decided to become followers, instead they have only chosen to work with this group of people to make the world a better place or to serve God. If you asked them if they had joined the group, they would tell you, no, they were just checking it out.

After people have been subjected to several weeks of mind control, they lose more and more of their ability to think logically, to feel their emotions, and act on those emotions in ways that make sense in the world outside the cult. The more they turn their decision-making ability over to the group leader, the less they are able to think critically about their decisions. Emotions are stuffed deep inside, and the only actions that group members take are those approved by the cult and its leadership.

According to Dr. Margaret Singer, a psychologist and college professor at Berkeley who has written extensively about the cult phenomenon, mind-control relationships are:

> those relationships in which a person intentionally induces others to become totally dependent on him or her for almost all major life decisions, and inculcates [instills] in these followers a belief that he or she has some special talent, gift or knowledge.

Singer and others who have made extensive studies of how cults remold members' behavior, deepest thoughts, and long-held values have discovered a number of mind-control tools used by cults to reform members and drive them to deeper and deeper levels of commitment to the cult and its beliefs. While a damaging cult may not use every single technique, most of them use several. When these tools are combined, they are extremely powerful.

- **The mind control programs are carried out on an uninformed person.** When Dr. Singer interviewed over 3,000 cult members who had left their groups, she found that not a single person set out to be involved with a guru or to violate their values. Instead, they felt they had been tricked into cult life. The Unification Church typically witholds the identity of its members, popularly called Moonies, from new recruits for three months. Because new members are spoon-fed information about the group so slowly, they often have burned so many bridges, there is no turning back when they do learn the truth.
- **Mind-controlling cults create situations in which the group dominates most of the person's thinking time.** This causes people to become passive. Members have little or no privacy. Whether cult members live in a community like the Branch Davidians or Synanon, or whether they join a group like Scientology or the Boston Church of Christ, their time is not their own. Every moment in the artificial world of the cult is filled with work, meetings, lectures, or other group activities.

All this busyness is not pointless. Some cults call putting new-found faith into practice or action by having newcomers in the group raise funds and help to indoctrinate other cult members *actionizing*. In some of the Multiplying Ministries groups, new members are placed in charge of even newer recruits within a matter of days after they affiliate with the cult. Such responsibility is flattering since it seems to indicate that leaders in the group have confidence in the new member.

- **Cult members are made to feel powerless.** The way they view reality is systematically attacked. Hours are spent being indoctrinated, listening to presentations of cult teachings. The idea that the beliefs and behaviors of the group will heal members and give them happiness and peace of mind is constantly stressed. As these messages are repeated many times, they become *internalized,* or taken inside, so that the belief becomes the cult member's own. In fact, he or she often forgets that belief wasn't always present.

Old patterns of behavior are broken as cult members learn new ways of eating, sleeping, speaking and even dressing. Sometimes these changes don't have much of anything to do with the cult's teachings. The important thing is that they separate the new member from his or her past and serve to split them further and further from former support systems of friends and family members.

A cult member's ability and desire to communicate with the outside world is limited. Even when members aren't forced to give up friends from the past and family, they often cut those ties after hearing over and over again that the cult is good and everyone else is bad. Followers internalize the teaching that they and other cult members are special, among the chosen. Outsiders are ignorant and maybe even doomed. Mom and Dad, who were seen as irritating, at worst, before, are now evil unbelievers. When parents express healthy concern over a son's or daughter's involvement with a cult, that worry is seen as the devil working through them to separate the cult member from salvation or enlightenment. People who used to be a cult member's best friends are viewed as fools because they don't subscribe to the group's belief system. Cult members are taught to fear outsiders, whom they are told, persecute members of the group.

- **Rewards and punishments encourage cult members to copy the way the leader and long-time group members talk and act.** Psychologists call this *modeling*. These rewards most often come in the form of praise. Members who follow the rules are told they are more "spiritual" or advanced than others. Praise can also be packaged as the sharing of secrets or a promise of being admitted to the cult's inner circle where members will be close to the leader and have power over others. During the California years of the Peoples Temple, members who acted like they were ill and had been cured during phoney faith healing ceremonies were given special privileges. One of the benefits of being admitted into the inner circle is the possibility of learning the real truth. Some experts term the secrecy characteristic of cult beliefs "split-level religion." One set of teachings is spoon-fed to new members, but only those who enter the inner circle have access to the real truth.

  Punishments may include public humiliation and the threat of being kicked out of the group. Some groups scapegoat a single member, carefully using that person's expulsion as an example of what can happen when people ask too many questions or break rules.

- **Control of members' time, splitting them from past support systems, and doling out rewards and punishments are all deliberately used to get rid of old beliefs and behavior.** Many cult leaders and inner-circle members claim to be able to read people's minds, when in truth they have a network of spies who report to them. Other groups stage fake healings, miracles, and exorcisms during which they claim to cast out demons. Nothing is what it appears in a damaging cult. Cult members often don't see that their loyalty is being forced because everything that happens in the day-to-day life of a cult is planned to appear as though it came about naturally—without any planning at all. Each experience is aimed at breaking the members' minds bodies, and spirits, and then reshaping them in the way the cult wants them to be.

- **Mind control requires a closed system of logic.** If group members are feeling miserable, they are told it is all their fault, not the group's. The member is told he or she is weak or doesn't believe deeply enough or, perhaps, possessed by evil spirits. Members are taught to stop questioning with what Robert J. Lifton, author of *Thought Reform and the Psychology of Totalism,* calls a *thought stopping cliche,* a phrase that brings members quickly in line. Some cults use Bible verses for this purpose. Others may simply use something similar to the "No pain, no gain," saying used by Synanon members.

- **Groups that use mind control have a rigid or *totalitarian* structure.** Life becomes one rule after the other. Communication flows from the top down, and cult members are taught to obey leaders without thinking. The group is the final judge of what is good and evil. The leader is always right because he or she is God's messenger on Earth—no questions, complaints, or changes are allowed. Members feel guilt and blame themselves when they don't agree or can't live up to the rules. As their self-esteem sinks lower and lower, they become more helpless and dependent on the cult for survival.

- **Mind-controlling groups place their doctrine or teachings over people.** Cult members are told that their individual needs are insignificant compared to those of the group. In fact, they are *nothing* without the group, which has the power to decide which people have the right to exist and which do not. Because the cult is the only group that knows the truth and can save members, group members soon believe that walking away endangers not only their lives on earth but will affect them throughout eternity. They would rather stay and face the unpleasant reality of cult life, than to risk being doomed or damned forever.

The Biology of Mind Control

Some scientists believe that one of the reasons mind-control tools work so well at changing beliefs and actions of followers is that some of these techniques may actually cause permanent chemical changes to take place in the brain. To understand this clearly, it's important to know a little about how the brain works to process information.

Our brains have over a hundred billion *neurons,* or nerve cells. These cells are shaped somewhat like spiders, with a main cell body and many tiny, thread-like structures branching from that body. These "legs" are called *dendrites.* The dendrites of one cell do not touch those of the next cell. When information travels from cell to cell in the brain it must pass across the gap between cells, which is called a *synapse.*

That information is carried by brain-manufactured chemicals called *neurotransmitters.* Endorphins, the neurotransmitters that make people feel good and lessen pain, are one kind neurotransmitter, but there are many others. Stressful life experiences as well as enduring weeks and months of hearing the same messages over and over again can affect the amount of neurotransmitters the brain releases and how those brain chemicals work to carry information.

According to recent research, if information is repeated often enough, the new information is chemically imprinted over the old, actually changing the pathways our thoughts follow. The biology of mind control may help account for the fact that people who join damaging cults change so dramatically and that those who leave cults often experience symptoms such as flashbacks for long after they break contact with the cult.

6

Take Me to Your Leader: Cult Leaders

The first two months Frank spent at the survival camp, he saw no trace of the group's founder, a mysterious man named Joseph, who had been born and raised in England. He kept to himself, Frank was told. Frank heard a great deal about him, though, and had listened to his taped lectures many times. Joseph didn't like meat or bright colors. These things had nothing to do with the group's teachings, and the members weren't forbidden hamburgers or vivid clothing, but all of them were vegetarians who limited the color of their clothing to black and brown. At least half of the people Frank encountered at the camp spoke with imitation British accents, even those who said they'd grown up in the Deep South. He had been puzzled—it seemed childish for people to try so hard to imitate another person.

When he was summoned to Joseph's cabin for a meeting, Frank was curious but skeptical. The instant he saw the man, though, he so was fascinated by the leader that he had to stop himself from staring. Tall and rugged looking, Joseph wasn't handsome but a mysterious air about him made him seem larger than life, as though he'd just stepped out of a movie. The atmosphere in the room changed, almost crackling with electricity. Before fifteen minutes passed, Frank found himself hanging on to every word that Joseph spoke. By the time his half-hour audience with the leader was over, Frank respected and trusted Joseph so much he would be willing to lay down his life for him if that were asked. He couldn't say why he felt such devotion to Joseph. The loyalty he felt didn't have anything do with what Joseph said to him. He just felt that way—more strongly than he had ever felt anything before.

Where do cult leaders like Joseph come from, and how do they gain such power? What gives them the ability to demand and receive total control over the lives of others? The answers to those questions are complex. Researchers have little understanding of the *inner* workings of the minds of cult leaders because the thoughts and feelings they show to others are carefully selected in order to add to their mysterious image as people chosen by God. It is possible, though, to learn quite a bit about cult leaders by looking at their lives and studying how they operate in the world.

One cult leader, Vernon Wayne Howell, was born out of wedlock in Houston, Texas, in 1958. Soon afterward, his mother moved to Dallas and raised him in the Seventh-Day Adventist church. A bright boy, he struggled in school because of dyslexia, a learning disability. By ninth grade, he became so frustrated that he dropped out. From then on his days were spent playing rock music on his guitar, studying the Bible, and memorizing lengthy passages of scripture.

When he was eighteen, Howell moved to the small town of Tyler, Texas. He attended the Seventh-Day Adventist church there, but the members didn't like the teenager's long hair or the way he dressed. Even when the congregation in Tyler kicked him out of their church, Vernon Howell clung to his religious beliefs. He began studying the teachings of the Branch Davidians, a small splinter group or sect that had broken off from the main Seventh-Day Adventist church and had settled outside of Waco, Texas in 1935 in a compound they called Mt. Carmel.

The Branch Davidians' founder had died in 1955 after predicting that the end of the world would come on Easter Sunday in 1959. His widow dissolved the sect that year when her deceased husband's prophesy didn't come true, but about fifty people continued to live at or near the compound after what they called "The Great Disappointment." A follower named Ben Roden took over the group's leadership until his death in 1978. Then Roden's widow, Lois, and her grown son, George, tried to run the group. By the time twenty-three-year-old Howell knocked on the door at Mt. Carmel in 1984, what had once been a strong organization was a wreck. George Roden claimed that he should be the leader, but the Branch Davidians didn't like him—many thought he was insane.

Vernon Howell told the Branch Davidian leadership that he had come for help because he was worried about his intense sexual feelings. Lois Roden, who was 67, began an affair with him. Soon, though, Howell and George Roden began fighting, and Vernon Howell was driven away from Mt. Carmel at gunpoint. He gathered a small congregation and they eventually settled in tents in Palestine, Texas, a small town near Waco.

When Howell got word that George Roden had dug up the body of a dead church member so that he could bring her back to life, he seized the opportunity to discredit him. Claiming that Roden had sexual relations with the body, Vernon Howell collected ammunition, gathered his people around him, and went to the compound for a shootout. The group was charged with attempted murder. After their trial, which resulted in a hung jury, charges against Howell and his followers were dropped. Even then, Vernon Howell had a magnetic personality— the jurors were so sympathetic to him that two of them hugged him when the trial ended, and he invited everyone in the courtroom to Mt. Carmel for ice cream.

Not long afterward, George Roden was sent to jail for contempt of court because of his behavior in an unrelated murder trial. Later he was sent to a state mental hospital after he was judged incompetent to stand trial for the killing. With George Roden out of the way, Vernon Howell began his life as a cult leader. He and his handful of followers started recruiting members in trips throughout North America, Britain, and Australia. He ended his affair with Lois Roden to marry a 14-year-old girl, the daughter of two Branch Davidians. Two years afterward, he said he had a revelation that God wanted him to have many wives like the biblical King David. Later he said he had another revelation that he was the seventh and last angel chosen by God to bring an end to the world. That time would come, he believed, when he moved to Israel and began to convert the Jews to his own faith; so he moved to Israel.

When the world failed to end by 1990, Vernon Howell moved back to Waco, changing his name to David Koresh. He chose the new name because *David* stood for King David, and *Koresh* was Hebrew for Cyrus, the Persian ruler who allowed the Jews to return to Israel. Next he began preaching to his followers that Armageddon, the battle that signaled the end of the world, would happen right in Texas. Believing himself a prophet, a king, an angel, and the new messiah, David Koresh began building bunkers and preparing those who had entrusted their lives to him for the final battle.

The Charisma Factor

David Koresh gathered loyal followers around him because he had a quality that psychologists call *charisma*. When people say that someone has charisma they mean that that person has a special ability to attract others. Most of the time when we talk about charisma, we are referring to a select group of actors, sports heros, political figures, and rock musicians. These special people have what old-time movie producers called *star quality*. They may not be better looking, more talented, or brighter than their peers, but people who possess charisma project an image that is hard for most of us to resist. These people gather fans so devoted, they are often called a *cult following*.

If a charismatic person walked over to us and shook our hands, we'd feel so overwhelmed, our hearts would start pounding. If someone with charisma asked us to do something, chances are we would do it in order to get that person's attention and approval. We would feel as though a little bit of the charismatic person's specialness had rubbed off on us. The closer we became to them, the better we would feel.

Some religious leaders have charisma, which helps them to attract a following larger and more devoted than possible through their teachings alone. Charismatic religious leaders are often treated by their followers as though they have supernatural, superhuman or, at the least, very exceptional powers. Simply being in the same room with such a person seems like a religious experience. Charismatic religious leaders also:

- promise followers salvation or enlightenment,
- are driven by an urgent sense of purpose, whether it is to save the world or guard against sin and corruption,
- feel that they have been chosen by God and may support this claim by saying that they have experienced visions.

Just because the leader of a religious group has charisma, doesn't ensure that he or she will end up heading a cult or causing harm to followers like David Koresh did. Buddha, Christ, Mohammed, and Moses are all considered to have been charismatic leaders or *enlightened teachers*. Their mission was to help people toward a closer connection with God. They had the power to attract a following and to get people to listen to and act on the messages they taught. This charisma helped them to establish the world's major religions.

Other charismatic religious leaders *do* cause harm to their followers. While charismatic leaders of the world's major religions tell believers that their most important relationship is between themselves and God, cult leaders teach that the relationship between themselves and their followers is the most important one. Charismatic cult leaders hold absolute power over their followers' lives. In addition to promising salvation, and having an intense sense of mission, harmful charismatic leaders:

- believe they are all-powerful, some to the extreme of thinking they *are* God;
- control and manipulate others without feeling guilt;
- think there is nothing wrong with hurting people as long as it helps them achieve their goals.

Because charismatic cult leaders claim to have God-given information that no one else has received, they claim to have a monopoly on the truth. The contents of these private revelations are usually fed to followers through lectures or writings called sacred texts. Followers believe leaders to have had visions and revelations even when they have no evidence of these occurrences. They feel that they can't challenge the rules their leaders impose on them because those rules are just as sacred as the visions and the charismatic leader.

Power Trips

Cult leaders cannot exist without the cooperation of followers who give them complete power over their lives. Were
it not for his handful of dedicated followers, David Koresh
would have been unable to wrest control of the Branch
Davidians from the Roden family or to raise the money to
amass his huge cache of weapons. The more loyalty leaders
build among members, the easier it is for them to accom-
plish their goals. Whether a cult grows into a huge business
empire or it dies shortly after it starts depends to a great
extent upon a leader's charisma and ability to take power.

Charisma, alone, gives leaders some power over others.
People look up to charismatic leaders, easily accepting
them as authority figures. Obedience to authority figures is
an automatic behavior pattern that most humans possess.
Four decades ago, Stanley Milgrim, a researcher from Yale,
was curious about why so many Germans followed Adolf
Hitler's orders and participated in the mass execution of
Jews and others during World War II. He recruited volunteers, telling them only that he wanted them to ask his
"research subjects" questions. If the answers they heard
were wrong, then they would need to shock the subjects
by running 195 to 300 volts of electricity through their
bodies. His helpers didn't know that Milgrim was really
studying them and that the people they had been asked to
shock were actors. Neither did they know that the wires in
his machine weren't hooked up.

Milgrim hoped that only a few people would hurt others
simply because they had been given orders to do so. His
hopes were false. His helpers "shocked" the subjects even
when the actors moaned, screamed, and twitched. Despite
the possible consequences, most of the helpers were more
than willing to inflict pain—all because a person in authority had told them to do it. Some became so upset that they
shook, but they still followed orders.

Bagwan Shree Rajneesh was a cult leader of humble origins who used his authority to whip his followers into such a loyal frenzy that they tried to take over an Oregon town. He began his career lecturing about meditation in India in the 1960s. Slowly, he began gathering a group of followers around him. In 1981 he moved to Oregon, and the next year he started a 64,000-acre commune called Rajneeshpurum near the small town of Antelope. There the guru shared his beliefs with 6,000 students. He taught that Jesus was a madman, that sex is fun and that he, Rajneesh, was the world's greatest lover.

The guru's followers were highly educated. An estimated 20% were mental health professionals and 15% to 20% had graduate degrees. Many were attracted to their spiritual leader because he seemed a rebel who made fun of people who thought they were important, like the leaders of organized religions and politicians. At the same time he criticized others for thinking so highly of themselves, Rajneesh bought ninety-three expensive Rolls-Royce cars. Everyday he would cruise through Rajneeshpurum in one of them, waving at his delighted followers.

After the Antelope Town Council began fighting the group over a zoning law, Rajneesh decided to take over the town by electing members of his group to seats on the city council. First he ordered thousands of street people bussed to Antelope from West Coast cities and registered them to vote. Armed guards patrolled the ranch to "protect" cult members. In reality, they were there to keep cult members in line.

Right before the election, some of the residents of Rajneeshpurum put *Salmonella*, a bacteria that causes food poisoning, in ten salad bars in The Dalles, a nearby city. Seven hundred fifty people became ill. The cult won the elections and changed Antelope's name to City of Rajneesh.

Four years later the guru's high opinion of himself made him careless, and his power began slipping. In 1985 a few cult members protested his activities by contacting police and telling them that Rajneesh and his assistants had broken the law, including plotting to murder people they considered enemies. A federal investigation charged the group's leadership with illegally trying to take over the county where they lived, and Rajneesh was arrested when he tried to leave the country. Before his trial, he plea-bargained the charge to immigration fraud and was deported to India. There he died of heart failure in 1990.

Grabbing for power can become a neverending cycle. The more power a cult leader has, the more he or she is tempted to take big risks. The stranger or more illegal a cult leader's behavior becomes, the more careful he or she must be to maintain complete control over members of the group. Charismatic cult leaders claim that they have authority from God to do whatever they want. Because they are holy men or women, they teach that they are above right and wrong.

Reward and punishment are two other tools cult leaders use to control their flocks. Leaders like David Koresh and Bagwan Shree Rajneesh understood that followers idolized them and believed they shared in the cult leader's power. Members' self-worth depends on how much attention they receive from the leader. Like an abusive parent, the charismatic leader of a destructive cult can shame his or her "children" with a harsh look or by ignoring them, or reward them by showing favoritism.

Some cult leaders deliberately structure their groups to resemble families, demanding to be called "Father" or "Mother" and treating followers like children. Jealousy and competition between "brothers" and "sisters" for a spiritual parent's approval and love becomes intense, causing members to try harder to bring in money and members in order to win the "parent's" affection. Reverend Moon is an example of a cult leader who has built a multi-million dollar "family" business called the Unification church.

When Young Myung Moon was born in rural northern Korea in January of 1920, the Japanese occupied the country, making life difficult for those who lived there. Moon was ten when his parents converted to Christianity and joined the Presbyterian church, taking their son to services. As a boy he was sensitive, crying over the sorrows of Jesus and throwing temper tantrums when he saw any child or adult being hurt.

On Easter morning when he was sixteen, Moon claims he saw a vision of Jesus, who told him that his own work had not been finished during the time He had lived on Earth. Jesus said that He had picked Moon to finish what He had begun, establishing His kingdom on Earth. In his biographies, Moon has claimed that over the next nine years he communicated with Jesus, Moses, and Buddha.

Eventually Moon studied engineering in Japan. There he claimed he had another vision, one in which he struggled satanic forces in the spirit world and won. Afterward he changed his name to Sun Myung Moon, which means Shining Sun and Moon.

When his studies were completed, he returned to occupied Korea at the age of 25. Moon was accused of trying to overthrow the Japanese occupation and was put in jail for four months. During his stay in prison, he had another revelation. This time he was told that he must chose between being a minister or being an engineer. Moon chose the ministry. After he was released, Moon left his family and began traveling throughout Korea to establish individual churches in the religion he had founded, the Unification church.

By this time Communists controlled northern Korea and were fighting to take over the south. Three years after Moon started his religious work, they arrested him and sent him to a prison camp. He stayed there for eleven years, writing *The Divine Principle,* a book outlining his teachings. Finally United Nations forces liberated the camp, freeing the Korean minister.

In 1959 Sun Myung Moon sent his first missionary to Japan. The next year he sent three to the United States. In the beginning his followers on this continent, the Moonies, numbered twenty members, most of whom lived in San Francisco. In 1962 those members were sent to establish churches near college campuses throughout California. The next year they were relocated to cities throughout the United States. In the meantime, Moon made three world tours, converting people to his beliefs and teaching against communism. In 1972 he claimed he had a revelation that urged him to move to the United States. There he began holding huge revival meetings.

The expenses of his ministry soared along with the church's membership. One eight-city tour of the United States cost a million dollars. In order to bring funds into the organization, Moon ordered his followers to begin spending long hours aggressively selling candy and flowers on the streets and at airports. With the money from these sales, Moon began buying property and making investments in ginseng (an Oriental herb sold in health food stores), titanium, and prescription drug manufacturing. Today the Unification church is reported to have over $200 million in assets.

Currently the Unification church has more than 6,000 believers in the United States and Canada. Moon has also started several political organizations that work to drive the Communists from Korea and Latin America. In addition to vast amounts of property in this country, the church owns newspapers and magazines including *The Washington Times.* During the past four years the organization has gained controlling interest in three independent Washington, D.C.–based video news companies that supply news clips to television stations around the world.

Sun Myung Moon's followers call the reverend and his wife "Divine Parents." According to the group's teachings, outlined in *The Divine Principle,* the proper relationship of human beings to God was destroyed in the Garden of Eden. God sent Jesus to restore the relationship, but His crucifixion came before He had time to finish His work. A second messiah was born in Korea in the 1920s. Although Moon's teachings don't name him as that messiah, he calls himself "Lord of the Second Advent" and his followers believe that he is the second savior of the world.

Moon rules his follower's lives so completely that he and his assistants tell people whom they can and cannot marry. In 1975 he united 1,800 Moonie couples in arranged marriages at Madison Square Garden. Despite his control, followers remain devoted to him. They have stood loyally by their "father" through a congressional investigation attempting to link him to South Korean attempts to bribe U.S. politicians. In 1984 Moon was convicted and jailed for income tax evasion. His $25,000 fine and 18-month sentence outraged the Moonies, who believed he was unfairly persecuted. Instead of feeling disillusioned and leaving the Unification church, they became more obedient to their "Divine Father."

The Power of Paranoia

Researchers have found that the demands and actions of spiritual leaders become most dangerously extreme when members face a crisis or threat to their well-being. (Lincoln and Mamiya 1980, Stern 1975). The more fearful followers become, the more they are willing to do anything to save themselves. If a leader can manipulate members to feel *paranoia,* or irrational fear, the leader's ability to control them increases dramatically.

L. Ron Hubbard was an eccentric charismatic cult leader who was able to use his own paranoia to build an organization even larger and more powerful than Moon's. Hubbard was born in Nebraska in 1911, served in World War II, and later complained to the Veteran's Administration that his mind had been "seriously affected" by the war. Years later he would lie, telling his followers that he had been a war hero who had been blinded in action, pronounced dead twice, and cured through Scientology.

Hubbard supported himself by writing science fiction and in 1950 published a book that formed the basis of his new religion. That book was called *Dianetics: The Modern Science of Mental Health*. Soon afterward he began offering classes and workshops based on his beliefs. Participants were charged high fees to be *audited,* checked out for signs of early trauma with a machine that resembled a lie detector. Auditing, Hubbard claimed, would make them mentally healthy. The catch was that the process, which cost as much as $500 an hour, never stopped.

By 1960 L. Ron Hubbard had disclosed a revelation that would later result in his making a great deal of money. People were made up of clusters of spirits that had been banished from the world 75 million years ago by a cruel intergalactic leader called Xenu, he said. All of these spirits needed to be audited, too. The fact that Hubbard's vision sounded like science fiction, didn't stop believers. Hubbard told them, "In all the broad universe, there is no other hope for man than ourselves. This is a tremendous responsibility. I have borne it too long alone. You share it with me now."

Scientology members now also shared their leader's fear that the government and the psychological community were out to get them. Scandals that have shaken the church since the 1970s when Hubbard was accused by the I.R.S. of skimming millions of dollars from the church have failed to make most Scientologists renounce their leader. When people who did drop out, including Hubbard's head of security, accused him of stealing $200 million from the church, followers responded by shredding documents in order to beat an I.R.S. rap for tax fraud. They believed both Hubbard and they were being persecuted. In the meantime, Hubbard retreated to his yacht and withdrew from personal contact even with his followers.

Despite the fact that Hubbard's wife and ten other key people in the organization were jailed in the mid-1980s for burglarizing and wiretapping over 100 government and private agencies in order to stop criminal investigations of themselves, Scientology today has 700 centers scattered throughout 65 countries. One division of the church alone, the Church of Spiritual Technology, reported $503 million in income in 1987. The Church of Scientology is also currently the focus of an F.B.I. racketeering investigation.

After Hubbard's death in 1986, the organization was taken over by David Miscavige who is the son of Scientologists and a high school dropout. Former Scientology members use words like *ruthless* and *cunning* to describe the new leader. Miscavige is reported to fear so much for his own safety that he keeps his water glasses covered with plastic wrap so no poison will get into them. It is reported that one of his pastimes is to shoot at pictures of people he has declared enemies with a .45 automatic weapon.

One would think that such unqualified leaders as Hubbard and Miscavige would have a difficult time running a huge organization. That is hardly the case. Since his tenure began Miscavige has hired Hill and Knowlton, a powerful public relations firm to clean up the group's image. One of the church's divisions, the Way to Happiness Foundation, has given public schools over three and a half million copies of a booklet that Hubbard wrote outlining his views on morality. Sterling Management Systems, which Hubbard founded in 1983, has recently been ranked as one of the most rapidly growing private companies in the United States by *Inc.* magazine.

Victimizers and Visionaries

Many damaging cult organizations are founded by leaders psychologists call *victimizers*. Because of an unstable childhood, a victimizer grows up learning to take advantage of other people by being able to sense their needs and then use those needs to control them. Many of the cult leaders discussed in this chapter are victimizers.

Some of the traits that characterize victimizer leaders are:

- feelings of alienation or separation from others,
- fears of any kind of loss,
- the need for complete control over other people and the world around them, and
- a need to blame other people when things go wrong.

In addition to being charismatic, victimizer leaders of damaging cults are *narcissistic*—they are in love with themselves and their own power. Leaders who fit the victimizer pattern can never have enough power or control.

Although a victimizer like David Koresh or L. Ron Hubbard may feel helpless, he or she acts self-confident. In fact, the victimizer's entire life may be an act. Because victimizers may not have a clear sense of right and wrong, they have no qualms about manipulating others.

Psychiatrist James Gordon, author of *The Golden Guru: The Strange Story of Bagwan Shree Rajneesh,* has studied a number of spiritual groups that have turned into cults. He has found that many of the groups that have transformed from helpful to harmful ones have sounded an apocalyptic note, their leaders preaching that the world would soon end.

Luc Jouret, a charismatic Beligian many of whose followers committed suicide, preached a combination of spiritual ideas and impending global disaster. According to a Swiss cult expert, Jouret had talked about pollution and the death of the rainforest. Jouret's gloomy predictions attracted between 150 and 200 followers in Europe and between seventy and eighty followers in Quebec.

Jouret told followers that fire was magical, but it was obvious he placed his faith in guns, as well. Last year two members of the Quebec branch of the Solar Temple were arrested and charged with conspiracy to purchase guns with silencers. Jouret, himself, had fled to Switzerland a year before the deaths of his followers after he pled guilty to conspiracy and weapons possession in Canada. Canadian investigators believed Jouret and his followers felt it was necessary to arm themselves for protection against the violence that would preceed the end of the world, which they believed would happen soon.

Some cult leaders may really have visions of the end or, at least, imagine a vision. A victimizer leader, however, will sometimes pretend to have a revelation of coming doom and deliberately use that lie to reduce followers to helpless puppets.

Jim Jones was a charismatic victimizer who used the visions he claimed to have to create a fear in his followers powerful enough to lead them beyond the brink of madness. Jones was raised in a small town in eastern Ohio. Like David Koresh, he had a difficult childhood. In his sermons, he described himself to his followers as a loner who lived on the edge of society. His father, a disabled veteran gassed in the First World War and a member of the Ku Klux Klan, according to Jones, had tried to drown his young son by throwing him off a bridge. Jones' mother, who worked in a factory to support the family, wasn't at home often. "I was deeply, deeply alienated," Jones later told his followers. "I was ready to kill." The authors of his biography *Raven,* write that once as a young man, Jones invited a friend to dinner. When the friend declined, saying he was leaving for home, Jones was so upset that he pulled out a gun and fired at his friend, narrowly missing.

In high school Jones worked as a hospital orderly and decided that he wanted a career in hospital administration, but already he was spending his spare time preaching on street corners. Right after Jones graduated from high school he married a woman he had met at the hospital. He eventually became a Methodist minister, but soon afterward he converted to Pentecostalism, and in 1956 he began the Peoples Temple in Indianapolis.

A dynamic speaker, Jones built a large congregation and turned his attention to helping others. First he integrated his congregation, encouraging people of all races to worship together. He opened a soup kitchen to feed the poor, which served three thousand meals a month. Members of the temple delivered coal to people who needed heat and provided them with food and clothing. Jones refused to draw a salary from his church, saying it would be taking money away from the poor. Instead, he supported himself by taking odd jobs. One of them was selling pet monkeys from door to door. A major supporter of the struggle for equal rights for blacks, in 1961 Jones was appointed to head the Indianapolis Human Rights Commission. Most people in Indiana thought Jim Jones was a compassionate man.

The turning point toward tragedy came well before the Jonestown Massacre when in 1962, Jones had a vision that the world would be destroyed by a nuclear blast and began searching for a safe place to live. He moved his family to Brazil and then to northern California in 1965. There he began teaching that his ideals would prevail over racist and corrupt societies that were fated to destroy themselves. This marked the start of a calculated campaign to boost his appeal and gain more power over the people who followed him.

Shortly after settling in California, Jones established a network of spies in his church. These people fed him information about everyone in the congregation as well as their relatives. When he felt someone was rebelling against him, he would call that person in for a talk. Before long people believed that Jones could read their minds. When the sick came to Peoples Temple asking him to cure them, he used that as a way to gain even more control. The "healing services" he staged were so impressive that people began to call his phoney powers "The Gift." The next act of the Jones drama would be the removal of his congregation to Guyana. Before the curtain came down most of his followers would die.

Ironically, victimizer charismatic cult leaders who predict the world's end, can't lose. Some of these leaders, like Jones and Koresh, provoke apocalyptic tragedies by deliberately breaking the law and then taunting authorities. When law enforcement people respond, the leader's predictions of doom are borne out. Those who survived Waco, for example, ignored the ways in which Koresh had engineered the end and became even more loyal to their dead leader, sure that he was an angel of doom.

Other cult leaders have predicted the end of the world over and over again, using that threat as an excuse to arm their organizations and to obtain a tighter grip over their membership. The dates they have set for the end have come and gone—yet obviously the Earth is still here. It would seem logical that the world having failed to end, followers would mistrust their leaders and leave the cult. If someone we respect is thrown in jail, we may rationalize what has happened by convincing ourselves he or she was set up or wrongly accused. When someone we respect insists they've had a revelation from God telling them that the world is going to end on a specific date and then it doesn't happen, making excuses for them becomes more difficult. Maybe God wasn't talking to that person after all. Maybe he or she is simply hearing voices and is insane. Could that person be taking drugs? Maybe our "prophet" made it all up. In the logical world most of us live in, serious doubts would be raised in our minds about trusting and respecting a false prophet.

The world of cults and cult leaders is not a logical one, however. Experts who have studied groups that believe the world will end soon tell us that the opposite is true—failed predictions cause respect and trust for a cult leader to skyrocket. When the world doesn't end, cult members like the Branch Davidians who endured "The Great Disappointment," face another crisis—that of being thought foolish by outsiders whom they have learned to consider enemies. After only a short time of turmoil, followers reorganize and rededicate themselves to their leader in order to fight against this humiliation. Many feel more loyalty to the group than they did before the crisis. Their loyalty makes it extremely difficult for them to leave the cult under any circumstances.

7

Getting Out

Over Christmas vacation Tina met the head of her friends' Satanic cult, a twenty-two-year-old dishwasher, who officially initiated her into the group, called a grotto. She wasn't impressed by the ceremony he made up—all he did was give a long speech. As it turned out, he hadn't actually met LaVey and had only read *The Satanic Bible*. Given the uneducated way he talked, Tina imagined he'd had a struggle finishing the book. Even so, being an official member made her feel closer to her friends.

Throughout the spring, she continued to write to them and the leader. In his letters, he said satanism would bring believers anything they wanted, but the harder she tried to live the way he urged, the lower her grades dropped. She couldn't concentrate on anything anymore—sometimes forgetting what classroom she was supposed to be in. Then horrible nightmares began invading her sleep and made her wake up screaming. Sometimes she cried for no real reason and couldn't stop. Maybe someone in the group had put a curse on her, she worried. Or maybe she was being punished by God for what she'd done.

After Frank spent weeks getting only four hours of sleep a night and eating a diet of starchy foods and sugar, he caught one cold after another. Instead of motivating him to take care of himself, sickness drove him to work even harder after Joseph told him that he was weak physically because he was weak spiritually.

When he reluctantly returned home at his parents' urging for a day-long visit, his mother was shocked at the skeleton her son had become. Frank had difficulty making the simplest conversation about day-to-day subjects. Whenever the discussion turned to the group to which he now belonged, he grew defensive. By now he couldn't even make minor decisions for himself. When his mom asked whether he wanted a sausage or pepperoni pizza, he couldn't answer; all he could do was stare into space.

The Walking Wounded: Cult Casualties

After weeks or months spent in a damaging cult, members begin to show signs of its harmful effects. These troubles persist for as long as the person remains in the cult and may continue from several months to years after leaving the group. The length and intensity of the problems depend on the length of time a person has spent in the cult and the intensity of the mind-controlling experiences he or she has endured during that time. Some of the scars cult members carry are described below.

Passivity

According to the Cult Awareness Network, people who have spent time in cults become passive. Because they are used to obeying rules and having others make all of their decisions, they forget how to think for themselves. Like Frank, they may be overwhelmed by simple choices about what to eat or what to wear. Their time has been so structured that they can't decide what to do themselves.

Their inability to control their lives may be so extreme that these people act in ways more appropriate to a young child, dependent on others to tell them what to believe. Cult researcher Dr. Margaret Singer calls this *uncritical passivity.* Cult members are so used to not thinking that eventually they tend to accept and believe everything they are told. Even after they leave a cult, they may mistake casual remarks for commands that need to be obeyed.

Loss of Spontaneity

Cult life and the black/white thinking that accompanies it forces members into very rigid patterns of behaving and thinking. Free time and unexpected events tend to make them uncomfortable. They no longer possess a sense of humor and have a hard time having fun. Often they have lost their ability to let go and laugh or even cry because they have learned to numb themselves from all feelings except those that cult leaders find appropriate.

Difficulty Forming Relationships

The inability of cult members to recognize and act on their emotions makes it very difficult for them to have close relationships. Sharing one's deepest thoughts and feelings with another person is dangerous in cults because it often results in punishment. As a result, people who have belonged to damaging cults for any length of time tend to hold themselves apart from others.

Good relationships demand a certain degree of flexibility. The give and take of compromising to meet the needs of both people in a friendship is hard for people who have become enmeshed in cults because it is so different from the rigid power structure they are used to.

Loss of Thinking Skills

When people spend time in damaging cults, their thinking suffers. Every aspect of cult life is aimed at preventing members from thinking critically. Cult members assume that everybody ought to share their opinions, and rarely can they find flaws in the cult's teachings.

Margaret Singer's studies of cult members show that they have difficulty concentrating and an inability to focus and maintain attention, as well as poor memory.

When Flo Conway and James Seigelman, research associates with the Project on Information and Social Change of the Communication Research Center at the University of Oregon, studied 400 former cult members in 1982, they discovered that more than half of them had experienced disturbances in perception and memory, especially short-term memory. It isn't surprising that cult life can also impair members' ability to communicate.

Severe Emotional Difficulties

Day-to-day life in a cult produces more and more psychological problems as members lose contact with the world outside. One of the signs of emotional illness that some cult members experience is hallucinations caused by sleep deprivation and malnutrition as well as constant bombardment by the tactics of mind control.

Paranoia, the mistaken belief that someone is out to get them, is another symptom some cult members experience. Feelings of paranoia are encouraged by cult leaders in order to bind members of their groups more closely. Some cult members develop phobias, intense and irrational fears, of anything that reminds them of the outside world or anything cult leaders label as sinful or unclean.

Guilt and low self-esteem cause other cult members to become very depressed and even suicidal. In rare cases, people who join cults have been reported to become psychotic, losing all connection with reality. Mind-control techniques make them so disoriented that they *completely* lose touch with who they are.

Illness and Abuse

Cult members frequently experience a number of stress-related illnesses, including ulcers, headaches, muscle pain and high blood pressure. Like Frank's, their immune system, the body's defense against disease, may weaken because of anxiety, lack of sleep, and poor nutrition so that they more readily catch colds and other infections than healthy people. The majority of former cult members in the

1982 Conway and Siegelman study indicated that they had experienced serious physical problems when they were cult members. Extreme weight gain or loss, abnormal skin conditions, and menstrual irregularities were common.

Other physical problems arise directly from mistreatment by cult leaders. This mistreatment can include physical beatings as well as malnutrition, overwork, and lack of sleep. Many recent court cases brought against cults reveal extreme physical abuse. For example in 1991, when she was taken to Flagstaff Medical Center after being involved in an automobile accident, Virginia Hayes, a 40-year-old blind woman from Flagstaff, Arizona told police that members of a small Christian fundamentalist group had beat her and tried to suffocate her as well as depriving her of food, sleep, and medical treatment. At the hospital, doctors found that her legs were infected and that she had gangrene in her hands and toes. For several weeks she was near death. Hayes informed the police that cult members had broken her bones during beatings that were intended to convert her. Cult leaders denied this, saying that Hayes had injured herself after men in the organization refused to have sex with her.

Sometimes cult members suffer physical abuse because the groups to which they belong place them in dangerous situations. As discussed earlier, raising money and gaining new members are more important to cult leaders than the health and safety of members. The Unification church has faced lawsuits from former members accusing them of physical abuse connected with fund-raising.

Breaking Free

There are three ways of leaving cults: *expulsion, exiting* and *extraction.* In an expulsion the cult expels, or kicks out, the member of the group. Exiting occurs when a member makes the choice to leave. Cult members who do this are sometimes called *walk-aways.* According to a survey of former cult members conducted by Dr. Michael Langone, director of research for the American Family Foundation, based on people who answered questionnaires printed in an anti-cult journal, thirty-nine percent of former cult members claim to have walked away from cult involvement without any kind of therapy or intervention.

When a cult member leaves the group by extraction, a concerned outsider, most often a family member, triggers that person's removal from the group. According to the Langone study, twenty-one percent of former cult members broke with their organizations after receiving voluntary counseling. *Deprogramming* is a coercive method of cult rehabilitation that uses physical force, including kidnapping and holding former cult members against their will. Forty percent of the former cult members responding to Langone's survey had been forcibly deprogrammed.

Expulsion

After Bonita disagreed with the speaker at the Bible study camp, she tried talking with the woman who had invited her. "The way people treat one another here doesn't seem very Christian to me," she protested. "It seems like people are always trying to condemn each other instead of loving each other like the Bible says people should do."

Bonita was told that the devil was working in her and that she should pray harder until she could totally accept the group's teachings and stop her questioning. At first she was angry, but soon she began to fear that her doubts really were caused by the devil and that she was an evil person for expressing them. She tried to do better, even after she discovered that the money the group said it was raising to help needy children was really going to pay for a $500,000 home for the group's founder.

Her rededication worked so well that after a while she was chosen to take responsibility for teaching new recruits. A few months later she was asked to start attending leadership-training meetings at the founder's luxurious home. There one of the group's leaders, a man at least three times her age, showed her a great deal of attention. Bonita was flattered and accepted his offer of a ride home. Over the next weeks, the two were together more and more often. When he told her that having sex with him would make her higher in the eyes of God, Bonita said yes. The fact that he was such an important person made her feel so special that it didn't really bother her when she found clues that he was sleeping with other girls in the group. For five months they carried on their affair in secret. All the time, Bonita was given more responsibility. Then she discovered she was pregnant.

When she told her lover she was going to have his baby, he ordered her to have an abortion, an act forbidden by the group's teachings. Shocked, Bonita told him that she would rather die than give up the baby. She was certain the founder would back her up, so she threatened to take the matter to him. "I'll tell them you're lying," the man insisted. "They'll believe me, but they'll never listen to you."

He was right. In a matter of days Bonita was summoned to a closed meeting where she was called a slut and a whore. The father of her baby smugly told her that she was a bad influence on those around her and ordered her to have nothing more to do with the group. The people who had once been her friends were ordered not to even look at her if they passed her on the street. Lonely and confused, Bonita accepted the decision. Part of her knew she wasn't as bad as they said. She'd made a mistake, but the cult leader who had become her boyfriend should have taken some of the blame. Another part of her felt like a worthless failure.

When cult members are expelled from their groups, usually it is because they ask too many questions, break rules or, like Bonita, do not obey direct orders. Some people are forced out of cults when they embarrass the group or cannot take care of themselves because of illness or emotional breakdown. Poor health may force them to stop working as fund-raisers or recruiters. Unable to bring money or new members into the cult, they are of no use to the groups that so intensely recruited them in the first place.

Often times expulsions are conducted in front of the cult's membership. Like the victims of the calculated humiliation at recruiting meetings, these people are used as scapegoats. Cult members who watch expulsions feel superior to the ones being kicked out. This binds group members more tightly together. Others fear that they will be the next target and vow to work harder at conforming to the group's rules.

Little research has been done on people expelled from cults, but it is known that these former cult members tend to feel a great deal of shame over the reasons for their rejection by the group. Many hide their time of cult involvement from others, suffering in silence.

Exiting: Walk-aways

Jamal continued to be involved with George's group throughout the remainder of the school year. Now he hung out at video arcades in order to talk total strangers into attending meetings, much like George had done to him weeks ago. When Jamal questioned the group's membership drive, he was told that once every teenager in the city joined, gangs would disappear—kids involved in the organization's activities had no time for gangs.

That was for sure! The nights and weekends Jamal didn't try to find new members, he sold candy door to door. He had no idea how the money he raised was being spent, just that the two to three hundred dollars he earned on a weekend was turned over to the leader. If he didn't sell enough, he was lectured about laziness in front of other group members.

He wished he could give his mom some of the money he was making; she needed a new refrigerator. For that matter, he could use some clothes and he wanted some tapes. There was no time for dating now or even shooting hoops with friends. He had to struggle to keep from failing in school, stealing a few minutes here and there to half-finish his homework.

One on top of the other, doubts slowly mounted in Jamal's mind. In the first place, he wanted some free time. In the second place, now that he was recruiting new members, he knew for a fact the friendliness he'd experienced from George and the other members was all an act. If the group leader told them to do it, his new friends would dump him in a minute.

More importantly, the group hurt people. One of another member's recruits, a skinny little thirteen-year-old girl who looked like she was ten and who said she had diabetes, had been driven to a suburban neighborhood early one Saturday morning and ordered to raise money. Like the other fund-raisers, she'd been ordered not to eat any candy and not to spend a dime of the money she'd made. By the time she'd been picked up after dark, she was dizzy and disoriented. Jamal, whose uncle had diabetes, knew she was well on her way to a diabetic coma. When he told the member driving the car that the girl needed some orange juice right away, he was told it was none of his business; the girl's dizziness was punishment for not working hard enough. When the driver got to her home, Jamal watched as he pushed her out of the car and onto the sidewalk.

For Jamal, this incident was the final straw. For days he felt terrible that he had done nothing to help the girl, and imagined how bad he would feel if he'd been the one to recruit her. There was no way he could stay with the group. It was probably as bad or maybe worse than being in a gang. He stopped going to meetings, and when members called him or stopped by the house to talk him into coming back, he told his mother to say he wasn't home. After a while they left him alone.

Cults don't make public the number of people who desert them. Researchers over the past decade have discovered that whether cults require their members to live in a common house or allow them the freedom of living at home or in their own apartments, large numbers of members do walk away. Some believe the number of walk-aways may be even greater than the thirty-nine percent cited by Dr. Langone's study. According to the Committee on Psychiatry and Religion of the Group for Advancement of Psychiatry, the majority of cult members join during late adolescence, but only one in ten current cult members is thirty-five years old or older, indicating that few recruits have remained in their groups over long periods of time.

Many cult observers believe that walk-aways usually leave their cults after about a year of membership. Like Jamal, they make their break once the effects of love-bombing wear off, and they become disillusioned with the reality of cult life. Others walk away from their groups when they realize that the cult isn't solving the problems that motivated them to join—the cult's easy answers to life's complicated dilemmas aren't really answers at all. Instead of making their troubles disappear, life in a cult gives members *other* troubles to deal with. In many cases these problems are worse than the ones they were trying to escape in the first place.

Some other reasons people walk away from cults are:

- a decision to marry the person of their choice and to start a family, something difficult to do given the strict rules of many cults;
- the choice to leave the group along with a spouse or significant other who has made the decision to walk away;
- ties with family members and old friends that haven't been completely cut—cult members feel lonely for their pasts and the people who were part of them;

- feelings of guilt and depression over actions the group has forced them to take that violate their values;
- "soft spots" in the conversion process that make cult members skeptical about how the day-to-day reality of cult life doesn't match the group's teaching;
- loss of faith in the cult leadership;
- contact with the outside world that weakens a member's ties to the cult;
- anger or feelings of failure from working extremely hard to help the group reach its goals but not being rewarded by being promoted to positions of responsibility in the cult.

What about cult members who stay? Do they enjoy cult life so much that they literally wouldn't walk away for the world? Experts believe that many people who stay in cults, no matter how difficult their lives become, do so because they have completely cut their ties with the outside world. Often their parents have rejected them because of the hurt they felt at having a child join a cult. Others have absolutely nowhere to turn for food, shelter, or clothing. When a cult member has nothing of value to take with them from the group and has nowhere to go that seems as though it would be better, it is easier to remain. If a member who walks away doesn't have a place to go, he or she may feel very unsure after leaving and return to the group after only a short time in the world outside of the cult. Finally, a number of cult members remain in their damaging groups out of fear, according to Margaret Singer. A number of cults use physical force to keep members from running away and use harassment and threats of physical harm against those who manage to escape.

Just as walk-aways have different reasons for leaving a cult, they use different methods of escape. According to cult researcher Stuart A. Wright, about forty percent of these departures are planned and are carried out in secrecy. More often than not, cult members who sneak off fear for their safety. Nearly half of the walk-aways are quiet, but open—the departing cult member packs his or her bags and calls home. The remaining percentage of walk-aways announce their departures to the group, stating openly their reasons for ending their involvement with the cult.

Wright found that most of those who snuck away had belonged to cults less than a year. Those who left openly but quietly tended to have been part of their groups for a longer time and had major disagreements with the cult's way of doing things. Probably they would have remained members if leaders had offered them a compromise. The former cult members who left openly and loudly had been involved with their groups for a long period of time and were so fed up with cult life and cult leaders that nothing could have convinced them to remain. They only wanted to get their grievances off their chest.

Even though many of the walk-aways in the Wright study were furious, only nine percent of them believed they had been brainwashed. The majority, sixty-seven percent, believed they were wiser for the experience. Their time spent as part of a cult had, at least, taught them what they *didn't* want from a religious organization. After leaving, they wanted to put the cult experience behind them and get on with their lives.

Extraction

Exit counseling, reevaluation, and family therapy are called noncoercive extraction. Although these kinds of treatment can sometimes place a great deal of emotional pressure on cult members in order to change their beliefs, these methods do not rely on physical force to separate members from their group or hold them against their will. Often noncoercive extraction gives cult members the moral support they need in order to say no.

In May when Tina's mom was cleaning the living room, she found a letter written to her daughter from one of her out-of-state friends. She didn't mean to read it, but as she folded it up to return it to Tina, the words *blood* and *evil* almost jumped out at her. Had Tina left the letter the on purpose so her mother would find it or had it merely dropped from her notebook? Tina's mom's hands shook as she read the page. She'd never imagined the strength of the grip the group of girls had on her daughter or the intensity of the nightmarish thoughts they were filling Tina with. Suddenly Tina's poor grades and crying all made sense.

At first Tina's mom was so angry, she wanted to take Tina's father to court in order to prevent Tina from visiting him again, but she knew that wasn't right. She wanted to talk to Tina, but she didn't know what to say. Unsure of the steps she should take, she called a psychologist who worked with adolescents and asked him for advice. He said that it was important for the teenager to stop communicating with her friends and the cult leader. It was also important that she start therapy.

When Tina came home from school and found that her mother knew about her friends and their activities, she was furious. "You can't stop me from writing to them," she screamed. "Yes, I can," her mom replied. "These people are hurting you. I love you and I have a right as a parent to protect you." Tina burst into tears. She had secretly been looking for a way to cut her ties with the group. Together, she and her mother cleaned her room, burning the letters and satanic books she'd saved.

She began attending sessions with the psychologist and slowly started feeling better. She'd made a mistake, he told her. It wouldn't do any good to waste time blaming herself—she needed to put her life back together. After a few sessions, the only thing that frightened Tina was the idea of seeing the neighbor girls again when she visited her Dad in the summer, but her psychologist promised he'd talk to both her parents and that together, as a team, they would work something out.

Frank's mother was so shocked at her son's health and behavior that she began attending parent support groups run by an anti-cult organization. At first she felt ashamed talking openly about her son's behavior, but in time, she began sharing the hurt she felt at her son's almost complete rejection of his family and the fear she felt for his safety.

One of the other concerned parents gave her the phone number of Paul, a man who specialized in deprogramming cult members. The techniques he used to "deconvert" cult members involved intensive information-giving sessions, lasting anywhere from days to months and designed to break down the member's new belief system. The woman who gave her the contact told Frank's mother that Paul was reputed to have a high success rate and then warned her that some of his methods were illegal.

When Frank's mom hired Paul, he told her to try and lure her son back home for his upcoming birthday with money Frank would want to donate to the survival camp. If Frank, suspicious of being deprogrammed, refused to come home and insisted on meeting his parents in a public place, that would be trickier, but it could be managed, Paul assured. True to the deprogrammer's predictions, Frank told his parents to meet him at a restaurant.

The day of the arranged meeting, Frank's parents were nervous, but determined to carry out their plan. Their hearts sank when they pulled into the restaurant parking lot and saw their son was accompanied by two other cult members, big men who looked like bodyguards. One of these men followed the family into the restaurant and the other waited outside the door. Frank's parents had been coached for such an eventuality, so Frank's mother protested the extra guest. When it looked like she might make a scene, the man gave up and stood with his companion outside the door.

Frank's family never did find out what happened to the two bodyguards—when they finished their meal and left the restaurant, the cult car remained where it had been parked, but the men were gone. Paul quickly appeared from around the corner of a building and gripped Frank's arm. When he tried to pull away, Paul twisted the boy's arm behind his back and steered him toward his car.

Frank was driven to a room in a remote motel where except for the times Paul's assistant brought them food or Frank had to use the restroom, he remained tied to a chair. Paul constantly criticized the cult and argued with Frank's beliefs in a loud voice. When Paul needed to catch a nap or eat, his helper took over. At the end of the four days, Frank didn't know what to believe any more. He only knew that he hated the survival camp and the people who ran it, and he was glad for having been saved from them. His parents were so grateful, they were happy to pay Paul the $5,000 fee he asked. They were lucky—some deprogrammers charge as much as $25,000. Others deprogram someone only to have that person return to his or her cult in a matter of days.

Did Frank have a right to continue his involvement with the cult, rather than being kidnapped and held prisoner, if that was what he wanted? He wasn't hurting anybody but himself. Should concerned family members be allowed to use force in order to remove a relative from a dangerous cult like the Branch Davidians or Peoples Temple? These questions are tough ones to answer. Even judges have had a difficult time sorting out the rights of people who belong to damaging cults.

The decade of the mid-1970s to the mid-1980s saw over 1,000 reported incidents of deprogramming in the United States, according to J. Gordon Melton, author of the *Encyclopedic Handbook of Cults in America*. During the 1970s the courts granted conservatorships, making parents guardians over their adult children, or spouses guardians over husbands or wives in order to allow the forcible removal of a loved one from a cult and the involuntary psychiatric treatment of that person by deprogrammers.

Deprogrammings have always been more popular in the United States than in Canada or European countries. However today, even in the United States, these techniques are on the decline. The United Nations Committee on the Protection of Minorities reported only about 500 deprogrammings occurred from the mid-1980s to today. Now fewer conservatorships are granted by the courts. They are given to concerned parents and spouses only when a judge has determined that the cult member is mentally ill and cannot care for his or her basic needs. Courts have generally upheld the freedom of adults to the religious beliefs of their choice that is granted under the Free Exercise Clause of the United States Constitution. Courts have also tended to uphold the rights of adults and minors to physical safety when cults have sued parents and deprogrammers, charging they violate the rights of cult members by physically assaulting them and holding them prisoner.

From the time the technique was developed by Ted Patrick in the 1970's, deprogramming has often been a violent process. In a book about his experiences called *Let Our Children Go,* Patrick describes how he and his assistant Lockwood once managed to separate one boy named Wes from his cult.

> Suddenly Lockwood grabbed the boy without warning and hurled him head first onto the seat. . . . Wes came bowling out to the street next to the car shrieking and waving his arms, shouting at the top of his voice 'Help! Help! they're kidnapping me! Call the police! Help me! . . .' I reached down between Wes's legs, grabbed him by the crotch and squeezed—hard. He let out a howl and doubled up, grabbing for his groin with both hands. Then I hit, shoving him head first into the back seat of the car and piling in on top of him.

Once the cult member is captured, deprogramming is usually performed in a room with the windows nailed shut, no phone, and the door locked from the outside. Sometimes when those who are being deprogrammed have tried to escape they have been handcuffed or tied to chairs as Frank was. Reports exist of deprogrammers having sex or giving drugs or alcohol to the people they are trying to deconvert. Guard dogs and guns have also been used to hold former cult members captive and persuade them to give up their beliefs.

Critics of coercive deprogramming feel that since so many deprogrammers are former cult members, who themselves have been deprogrammed, instead of trained mental health professionals, the possible damage they do is great. A former cult member may be deprived of food or sleep until he or she "breaks" under the pressure and admits to being wrong. Even when deprogrammers don't kidnap cult members or hold them against their will, some mental health professionals believe that the intense confrontation and information-giving sessions of deprogramming can be as traumatic as physical rape in some cases. Often deprogrammers tell former cult members that they were brainwashed into joining the cult. This allows former members to see themselves as victims who must accept everything the deprogrammer tells them as being true. Some mental health professionals believe that it also may explain why far more deprogrammed former cult members report being brainwashed by the cult than do walk-aways.

In addition to legal and ethical reasons, coercive deprogramming may also be losing popularity because there is little solid evidence that it consistently works. When psychiatrists J. Thomas Ungerleider and David K. Wellish studied cult members who had been deprogrammed, they found that the technique worked reliably only on people who had been involved with cults for a year or less. According to the 1984 study done by Michael Langone, thirty-seven percent of those who claimed to have been deprogrammed eventually returned to the groups from which they had been snatched.

Some people believe that deprogramming shouldn't be used because, unlike cult recruiting, it fits the definition of brainwashing, especially when it involves physical force. Ungerleider and Wellish claim that the techniques of deprogramming only reprogram the cult member back to his or her previous belief system, rather than freeing that person to make a rational choice. When a former cult member who is being deprogrammed refuses to give up cult beliefs, the deprogramming is seen as a failure, not a choice.

Life After the Cult

No matter how cult members leave a damaging group, most of these people suffer effects of cult life long after their contact with the group has stopped. Dr. Margaret Singer, who over the past twenty years has studied more than 3,000 people who have been subjected to mind control, has found that most former cult members feel a sense of alienation and confusion. Their confusion results from their previously held values, goals, and rules for living having been weakened. When they reenter the world outside the cult, they often feel like refugees entering a new culture.

Many former cult members have lost old friendships, and even when the bonds of friendship are renewed, the people they were close to before may have moved or married. Former cult members often feel as if they have nothing in common with the people they were once close to. Frequently their families act differently toward them and have a hard time understanding and accepting their absence.

Making matters more difficult are the changes in music, T.V. shows, and fashions. Many former cult members have spent months or years being so cut off from the outside world, they aren't aware of major news events or changes in popular culture that occurred during their time away. It is impossible for them to go back to the way life was before the cult because the past no longer exists.

In addition to dealing with changes in the world, they need to learn to cope with the many changes cult membership has made in how they think and feel about themselves. Because conversion happens so quickly, many members repress, or hide from themselves, the personality they had before joining—instantly taking on new ways of seeing and being in order to survive. The new cult beliefs don't become an integrated part of themselves and are sealed off or fragmented. Once a member's days with the damaging group have ended, he or she must put together the split or doubled self maintained in the cult and come to terms with who they are.

This can be difficult to do without professional help because life in a cult trains people to completely deny their pasts. Many former cult members try to get on with their lives, blocking off all conscious memory of the cult experience much as they buried their past personalities when they joined the cult.

No matter how hard an ex-cult member tries to adjust to life after the cult, most experience something called *floating*—an altered state of mind much like a drug flashback during which the person is involuntarily snapped back into a cultic state of mind. When ex-cult members talk about floating, they say they feel as if they are in two worlds at once. Others report thinking they are losing their minds. Floating episodes occur because the person's identity has become so fragmented. According to Dr. Singer, these floating episodes happen most frequently right after someone leaves the mind-controlling group but can go on for up to two years. Stress, tiredness, depression, or even words or ideas that remind a person of the cult from which he or she came can all trigger floating.

Most former cult members also experience something called *PTSD* or *post-traumatic stress disorder,* a collection of symptoms that occur after *trauma,* an event that severely jars the mind or emotions. Often cult life is a day-to-day collection of such traumatic events. People who suffer post-traumatic stress disorder are *hypervigilant,* always alert to danger. They may have an exaggerated startle response. If someone quietly comes up behind them, they panic. They have a difficult time sleeping and may be extremely moody. Often people with PTSD feel emotionally numb most of the time, a strategy they use in order to get through the crisis.

Because each former member is different and because his or her cult experiences weren't the same, their problems differ when they reenter the world they once left behind. It is safe to say, however, that the vast majority do have problems. Some other difficulties that former cult members have reported are:

- a sense of meaninglessness,
- regret for the time they lost while cult members,
- emotional breakdowns that may last from one to five months,
- anxiety and panic attacks,
- anger at themselves and the cult,
- guilt over things they may have done as cult members and at leaving others behind to suffer the group's abuses,
- grief over the friends left behind in the cult,
- shame and low self esteem,
- mistrust of people or groups,
- loneliness and isolation.

Many former cult members refuse to talk about their lives in damaging groups and some refuse even to admit they belonged to cults. They try to forget their lost years, burying anger, fear, and pain deep inside. Sometimes families and former friends make matters worse by being judgmental, instead of accepting and supporting the person who has returned. They may even believe the former cult member is sick or stupid. As a result, many cult members practice denial. Although people in denial may appear fine on the surface and for a short time, they are not healing. Eventually the act falls apart.

Healing from Cult Abuse

Over the past few years a number of counselors and psychotherapists have begun looking at how people can be helped to recover once they leave cults. Some of these specialists call themselves *exit-counselors*. Even though former cult members have many problems, they can be healed by working with a trained exit counselor or a good therapist.

According to Carla Pfeiffer, former director for the Norfolk Enrichment Center, a facility that helps former cult members heal, the amount of therapy required by former cult members depends on how long they spent in the cult, their physical condition when they left, and the amount of time spent in intensive indoctrination exercises. Other experts believe that strong family ties help a former cult member to recover more quickly. Most agree that it takes former cult members time and patience to readjust—expecting them to just "snap out of it" isn't realistic.

One of Dr. Margaret Singer's former-cult-member-clients once explained to her,

> People just can't understand what the group puts into your mind, how they play upon your guilts and needs. Psychological pressure is much heavier than a locked door. You can bust a locked door in terror or anger, but chains that are mental are hard to break. The heaviest thing I've ever done is leaving the group, breaking those real heavy bonds on my mind.

Before former cult members can break their mental chains, they must examine the rollercoaster of emotions they ride when they first leave the cult. According to researcher Willa Appel, "Shame is one of the invariable consequences of cult involvement." It can also be the most crippling emotion former cult members face. People feel stupid for having joined cults and they are ashamed that they would let themselves be humiliated within the group. They also may be ashamed at having brought other people into a cult or about other things that they've done to hurt people during their cult involvement.

Without the guidance that therapy provides, some former cult members avoid facing and healing their shame through overwork, drinking, or sexual adventures. Others run away from adjusting to the world by joining another group that prevents them from having to take responsibility and make choices. Wright's study showed that seventy-eight percent of those who left cults soon made some commitment to another belief system, more than half of those people became involved in rigid versions of Christianity with authoritarian power structures and many rules. For this reason some counselors encourage their clients to take a temporary break from the spiritual search.

Another challenge of former cult members is that of learning how to regain the social skills and self-confidence to build relationships. Even interactions as simple as shopping for groceries and clothing, going to the movies, and eating at restaurants require skills that ex-cult members may have forgotten and confidence that they may not be able to muster. Chatting with a friend on the telephone or going out on a date can be overwhelming. Usually exit-counselors urge their clients to practice these tasks one small step at a time.

Once former cult members can function in the world again, they are faced with weathering life's transitions and solving the problems that made cult life tempting in the first place. According to Margaret Singer and other cult experts, most of the people who pledge allegiance to mind-controlling groups in their teens and leave in their twenties often seem frozen at the level of emotional maturity they had reached when they joined. Not only were their lives interrupted by dropping out of school or quitting work when they became part of a cult, their emotional growth toward adulthood stopped as well. These former cult members often need long-term support to provide them with encouragement.

Not so long ago, many mental health professionals were reluctant to help former cult members or even to admit that they needed help. Out of ignorance, they thought that cult membership was just a fad or a stage that very few people went through. Others accused former cult members' parents of having severe emotional disturbances and former cult members of being highly disturbed for having joined damaging religious organizations.

In response, many former cult victims took matters into their own hands by starting self-help groups throughout North America. These groups share information, make referrals to trained mental health workers sympathetic to the problems of former cult members, and provide emotional support. People who have left cults use self-help organizations to connect with others who have suffered similar experiences and who understand what they are feeling. Often they are able to help others, which furthers their own healing as well. Some self-help groups for former cult members are listed in Chapter 9 of this book.

When a Family Member or Friend Joins a Cult

Most people who know someone who has joined a cult want to help, but often they don't know how. Sometimes they feel ashamed of their friend's or relative's cult membership. At other times they may feel guilty, believing that they must have done something very wrong to push someone they care about into a damaging group. When cult members reject their past, family members and friends often react with bitterness, angrily rejecting the cult member to pay that person back for the emotional hurt they're feeling. Other friends and family members fear for their loved one's safety and act unwisely out of panic. Shame, guilt, anger, and fear all drive concerned family members and friends to do all the wrong things in order to "help" the cult member.

To truly aid a cult member, family and friends need to remember that not all cults are destructive. Dr. Michael Langone advises that there is no recipe or formula for talking someone into leaving a cult. Grabbing at the first strategy that comes along rarely works.

Although rescuing someone from a destructive cult or talking them into leaving usually fail, several things *can* be done to help cult members. Among them:

- Keep lines of communication open with the cult member. If that person writes to you, answer his or her letters. Offer invitations to visit. Accept phone calls, even collect calls. No matter how frustrated you become, do not end your relationship with that person. Instead, keep reminding yourself that having a good support network in the outside world ultimately raises the chances of the cult member deciding to leave the group.
- When you talk to the cult member, listen to what he or she says and show interest. Be open minded and calm, rather than condemning the person or making a scene. Remember that cult leaders teach that outsiders are enemies. If you act like your friend's or family member's enemy, you confirm the damaging cult leader's teachings.
- Don't call the cult member names or say that he or she is stupid. Try to limit your use of words like *brainwashing* and *cult,* which will cause that person to stop listening to you.
- Don't get caught up in arguments about whether the group is good or bad or in arguments about its teachings. You can't win. The cult member is convinced that his or her group is good and that its teachings are true. The cult member has also been trained to use thought-stopping techniques if any doubts arise.

- Never try to bribe the cult member or to threaten, order, or punish that person. It is okay to firmly express your concerns as long as you focus your criticism on the group's actions such as manipulation and lying.
- Instead of blaming the cult member for your own negative feelings about their group affiliation, share these feelings by using "I" statements. "I feel really hurt that you have rejected me."
- Respect the person's desire for a spiritual life. Just because your friend or family member chooses to join a group that you wouldn't join or to believe a set of teachings you wouldn't believe in, doesn't mean that their choice is stupid, silly, or damaging.
- Find out as much as you can about the cult by reading its literature. You might want to read magazine and newspaper articles on the group or contact some of the resources listed in the back of this book. By becoming informed, you can better talk with the cult member and also have a better idea whether your concern for the safety of that person is justified.
- Try to have as little contact as possible with the group and its members. No one is immune from unfair persuasion and mind control. Sometimes people, like Frank, who try to rescue cult members, wind up becoming cult members themselves.
- If you need help, find a professional who knows about cults and who does not use illegal methods to remove the member from the group. Checking out the person's credentials is important because some people who call themselves deprogrammers or exit counselors do not have professional training. Some are former cult members dealing with their anger and shame by trying to save current members. Others may simply be people taking advantage of parents' and family members' fear in order to charge large amounts of money for deprogramming, therapy, or legal action.

8

Resisting Cult Involvement

If Jamal, Bonita, Frank, and Tina had known the truth about damaging cults and how to stand up to cult recruiters, they could have avoided a great deal of emotional pain. As it was, they knew very little because few people are willing to talk straight about cults, and few people are willing to listen. That's because most people believe cult involvement could never happen to them.

Could you possibly join a cult? To check out your chances, on a piece of paper answer the following questions?

1. Do people think of you as being smart?
2. Once in a while do you like to take a chance?
3. Are you interested in exploring new ideas and curious about the world around you?
4. Do teachers and friends consider you to be a leader?
5. Do you take part in after-school activities?
6. Do you cooperate well in groups?

7. When you look at the world around you, do you worry about your future sometimes?
8. Do you want to make the world a better place?
9. Once in a while do you have doubts about your worth as a person?
10. Do you feel good being with people you like and especially good when they let you know how much they like you?

If you can answer *yes* to at least three of these questions, then you are a prime candidate for a cult. Judy Israel, a contributor to the book, *Cults and Consequences* published by the Jewish Federation Council of Greater Los Angeles, warns, "All that is missing is the right time, place and a recruiter from a cult."

Since leaving a cult is difficult, wouldn't you rather avoid joining one in the first place? Just because you may be candidate for cults, doesn't mean there's nothing you can do to avoid them. Resisting cult recruitment is fairly easy—*if* you know what to look for and what to do. If you find yourself in the "right" place at the "right" time and a cult recruiter just *happens* to be there, the following practical tips can help you resist unfair persuasion.

- Remind yourself that even though you are smart, you *aren't* immune from cult recruitment. Admitting your vulnerability helps you keep your emotional defenses raised and your thinking critical.
- Take the time to become informed about cults by reading books and articles and by watching T.V. specials.
- Learn about spirituality and different religions. When you understand terms like *born again, enlightenment, karma* and *salvation,* you are less likely to accept a cult re-cruiter's explanations as correct.
- Stay aware of the social conditioning everyone raised in our society grows up with. When you know that an automatic behavior pattern like reciprocation strongly

affects how you will react to a cult recruiter's manipulation, you can avoid putting yourself in situations where you will feel obligated. If you're aware of your natural tendency to obey orders given by a person who seems to be in authority, you have a choice rather than doing what you are told without thinking.

- Resist the social pressure to conform by remembering it is your right to say *no*. Advises psychiatrist Philip G. Zimbardo, an expert on fighting manipulation, "Be willing to disobey simple situational rules when you feel you should, to sound false alarms occasionally or cause a scene. Never do anything you don't believe just to appear normal or to get someone off your back."
- Stay alert to the differences between what people claim to believe, and how they actually act in the daily course of their lives. Nobody's perfect, but if those differences are big ones—beware.
- Practice critical thinking by looking for *logical fallacies,* or flaws in reasoning. If a cult recruiter presents you with a false dilemma, forcing you to choose between two things like joining the group or going to hell, mentally add another alternative to the equation—none of the above.
- Don't make life-changing decisions when you're hungry, tired, angry, feeling sorry for yourself, or stressed out. We all have our weak moments. If a cult recruiter puts you on the spot, tell that person you'll get back to them later.
- Unless you're certain who is sponsoring it and what is going to happen there, don't accept an invitation to a seminar, retreat, or class, especially if the offer seems too good to be true. Before you commit to anything, ask the advice of an adult you know and trust.
- Look for hidden agendas. If you have a sneaking suspicion that information about the true purpose of what's happening is being kept from you, pay attention to that feeling.

- Ask questions—and don't settle for vague answers or appeals to your emotions that aren't answers at all. Learn to spot evasions like, "You're too stupid to understand," "Once you've attended a few more meetings, you'll catch on," or "It's mystical and can't be put into words."
- Recognize flattery and phoney instant intimacy—people rarely become best friends after only a few minutes of conversation. At the same time, resist revealing too much about yourself to other people too soon. If you show your weak spots to a cult recruiter, he or she won't hesitate to take advantage of the situation.

The strongest weapon against manipulation by cult recruiters or anyone else, for that matter, is self-knowledge and healthy self-esteem. If you know who you are and what you believe in, you are less apt to be talked into violating your values. If you take it a step further and know what you *don't* like about yourself, you can be aware when a cult recruiter is manipulating your weaknesses. Then you have a choice to accept the cult recruiter's solution or to look for other ways to solve your problems.

If you find yourself in a situation you can't leave and a cult recruiter's manipulation is causing you to feel bad about yourself, Dr. Zimbardo suggests that you think about the things you do well. Another tactic that works well is to picture people and things you care about. Thoughts such as these help keep your inner core of self-esteem from being violated. If someone tries to convince you to attend a meeting or workshop by telling you that you'd be foolish to refuse, ignore the word *foolish* and substitute the word *different*. It's okay to be different. It's okay to be yourself.

Spotting the Good Groups

Knowing what a *healthy* religious or self-help organization is like is just as important as being able to spot the danger signs of cults. Positive groups remind us that we are in charge of our lives and the decisions that make them up. Positive organizations claim to offer guidance, encouragement, and tips on techniques, not magical solutions to our problems. Both group leaders and members are able to laugh, displaying a sense of humor instead of the air of grim disapproval that surrounds many cults. People involved with legitimate organizations act with confidence and sensitivity rather than self-importance or arrogance.

Growth-promoting circles encourage understanding of and unity with people of other beliefs. They respect the individuality of members and of those who don't belong to the organization, as well as respecting every individual's right to make choices. If a group encourages critical thinking and allows for differences of opinion, if members are encouraged to compromise in order to find solutions that allow both sides to win rather than using violence and manipulation, chances are it is a healthy one.

Before you join any organization, you might want to ask yourself the following questions:

- Are you accepted for yourself or are you asked to condemn your past and to make extreme changes in your beliefs in order to become a totally new person? When people make these complete changes, does the group take it as a sign of spiritual progress?
- Does the group have a large number of rules? Are members severely punished if they break them?
- Are members forbidden or discouraged from expressing opinions different from the leader's, from asking questions, breaking rules, or contact with the outside world?
- Does the group make it difficult to place phone calls or to visit your parents or old friends?
- Are outsiders considered to be the enemy?
- Are you allowed to have privacy as well as adequate food and sleep?

- Do group leaders try to control your personal, ethical, financial, and political decisions by imposing guilt trips or trying to sexually manipulate you? Is dropping out highly discouraged?
- Are you encouraged to donate large amounts of money or to ask others for donations? If so, do you know how the group's money is being spent?
- Are you told that it's okay to lie to people or to steal in order to help the group?
- Do the group's leaders live by one set of rules and the followers live by another, stricter set?
- Have you been told that the leader can perform miracles? If that is the case, have you actually seen those miracles or are they revealed only to people in the inner circle?

The best protection you have against joining a cult is your critical thinking ability. The knowledge you've gained from reading this book combined with your own intelligence won't make you immune to cult manipulation, but they will give you the power to avoid dangerous groups before they have a chance to entrap you.

9

Where to Go for Help

The following organizations provide information about cults and help former cult members to recover from life in a damaging religious group. Because so many smaller self-help groups that deal with issues relating to involvement with a specific cult are informally organized, information about how to connect with them changes often. We have tried to be as up-to-date as possible.

American Family Foundation
P.O. Box 2265
Bonita Springs, Florida 34133
(941) 495-3136
(212) 533-5420 (New York office)

Christian Research Institute
P.O. Box 500
San Juan Capistrano, California 92693
(714) 858-6100

COMA
Council on Mind Abuse
P.O. Box 575
Station Z
Toronto, Ontario
Canada MSN 2Z5

Maynard Bernstein Resource Center on Cults
Jewish Federation of Greater Los Angeles
6505 Wilshire Boulevard
Suite 802
Los Angeles, California 90048
(213) 852-7864

Cult Clinic
Jewish Board of Child and Family Services
120 West 57th Street
New York, New York 10019
(212) 632-4640

InfoCult
5655 Park Avenue
Suite 208
Montreal, Quebec
Canada H2V 4H2
(514) 274-2333

Personal Freedom Outreach
P.O. Box 26062
St. Louis, Missouri 63136
(314) 388-2648

Religious Movement Resource Center
629 South Howes Street
Fort Collins, Colorado 80521
(970) 490-2032

Watchman Fellowship
P.O. Box 530842
Birmingham, Alabama 35253
(205) 871-2858

For Further Reading

The following books will provide further information on cults.

Beit-Hallahmi, Benjamin. *The Illustrated Encyclopedia of Active New Religions*. New York: Rosen Publishing Group, 1993.

Cohen, Daniel. *Cults*. Brookfield, Conn.: Millbrook Press, Inc., 1994.

Ottens, Allen. *Coping with Satanism*. New York: Rosen Publishing Group, 1993.

Ross, Terry. *Cults*. Vero Beach, Fla.: Rourke Corporation, 1990.

Stevens, Sarah. *Cults*. New York: MacMillan Children's Book Group, 1992.

INDEX